APPLIED MATH SKILLS

Decimals

CAMBRIDGE ADULT EDUCATION
A Division of Simon & Schuster
Upper Saddle River, New Jersey

Executive Editor: Mark Moscowitz
Market Manager: Will Jarred
Project Editors: Karen Bernhaut, Douglas Falk, Amy Jolin, Kristin Shepos-Salvatore
Editorial Development: Pat Cusick & Associates
Production Editors: Alan Dalgleish, John Roberts
Interior Design and Electronic Page Production: Lesiak/Crampton Design, Inc.
Cover Design: Pat Smythe

Printed in the United States of America

1 2 3 4 5 6 7 8 9 10   99 98 97 96 95

ISBN 0-835-94628-2

CAMBRIDGE Adult Education
A Division of Simon & Schuster
Upper Saddle River, New Jersey

CONTENTS

TO THE LEARNER

The books in the Applied Math series are designed to help you understand and practice math skills. Lessons are easy to use, and the problems demonstrate how math is used in the workplace.

Lessons have the following features:

- Every lesson is based on a problem encountered in the workplace. You are asked to use your knowledge of math to find a solution.

- The *Words to Know* sections introduce you to important terms and symbols as you begin each lesson.

- The *Example* sections show you how to use the skills presented in the lesson. The *Example* shows each step of the problem and gives you an easy-to-read explanation of the computation process.

- The *Exercise* sections give you a chance to practice new math skills gained from the *Example*. Every *Exercise* includes an *Application* question that allows you to use these skills in a new workplace problem.

- The *Math Tip* sections provide summaries, suggestions, alternative problem-solving strategies, and aids to help you remember and apply selected skills from the lessons.

- The *Use What You Have Learned* sections review all the math introduced the lesson's *Examples*. The *Applications* combine new skills with skills previously learned to solve problems drawn from a variety of workplaces.

Each chapter of each book contains a *Summary* and *Math at Work* section to help you judge how well you have mastered the chapter's material. The *Summary* reviews the math skills taught in the preceding chapter. *Math at Work* contains workplace problems that require the learner to use all of the skills taught to that point in the book. The *Answer Key* section at the end of the book provides answers, worked-out solutions, and explanations of how the problems can be solved. Answers are printed in color to make them easy to find. Use the worked-out solutions to see where errors occurred or to compare your successful approach to a problem with the author's.

The lessons in this book are designed to help you gain increased confidence in your math skills and to show you the practical value of mathematics in your working life. Good luck.

CHAPTER 1

Introduction to Decimals

LESSON 1   Decimals and Fractions

Faye was recently promoted to assistant supervisor of her department. She and the workers in her department sew pockets onto men's shirts. They are paid $45.00 per hundred pockets sewn. Faye has been asked to keep track of the number of pockets each of the five workers complete and to record the number of pockets shown in decimal numbers.

Date	Worker's Name	# Pockets	Fraction	Decimal
8/23/96	Marta	60	60/100 = 3/5	.60
	Elmer	75	75/100 = 3/4	.75
	Bill	25	25/100 = 1/4	.25
	Susan	60	60/100 = 3/5	.60
	Jasmina	80	80/100 = 4/5	.80

Decimals

A decimal is a number with a decimal point in it. It is another way to show a fraction or a part of something. Like a fraction, a decimal can be another way to show a value less than one. Here is a fraction/decimal equivalency chart.

Fraction/Decimal Equivalency Chart

# Pockets	Fraction	Decimal	# Pockets	Fraction	Decimal	# Pockets	Fraction	Decimal
50	1/2	.50	17	1/6	.17	38	3/8	.38
33	1/3	.33	83	5/6	.83	63	5/8	.63
66	2/3	.66	14	1/7	.14	88	7/8	.88
25	1/4	.25	28	2/7	.28	11	1/9	.11
75	3/4	.75	42	3/7	.42	22	2/9	.22
20	1/5	.20	57	4/7	.57	44	4/9	.44
40	2/5	.40	71	5/7	.71	56	5/9	.56
60	3/5	.60	86	6/7	.86	78	7/9	.78
80	4/5	.80	13	1/8	.13	89	8/9	.89

EXAMPLE 1

Marta sewed 50 pockets

Look at Faye's problem.

Step 1 Faye creates a fraction by placing the number of pockets sewn over 100.

$$\frac{50}{100}$$

Step 2 She then reduces the fraction to its simplest form.

$$\frac{50}{100} = \frac{1}{2}$$

Step 3 Looking at the Fraction/Decimal Equivalency Chart her supervisor gave her, she sees that 50 sewn pockets is the equivalent of $\frac{1}{2}$ or .50 of a job lot.

$$\frac{1}{2} = .50$$

Step 4 She records .50 next to Monday on Marta's pay worksheet.

Date	Worker's Name	# Pockets	Fraction	Decimal
8/24/96	Marta	50	50/100 = 1/2	.50

EXERCISE 1

Using the Fraction/Decimal Equivalency Chart above, write the decimal equivalents for the following workers in Faye's department.

1.

Date	Worker's Name	# Pockets	Fraction	Decimal
8/25/96	1. Marta	71		
	2. Elmer	57		
	3. Bill	78		
	4. Susan	80		
	5. Jasmina	66		

APPLICATION

2. Yolanda works in a camera store and is in charge of selling film. There are 10 rolls of film in a brick. A customer wants .50 of one brick of Tri-X black and white film and .40 of a brick of color film. How many rolls of each kind of film should she put aside?

Check your answers on page 99.

MATH TIP

While you will later see that conversion between decimals and fractions is a relatively simple matter, you will find it helpful to memorize the decimal equivalencies listed in the chart produced above. Knowing these equivalencies can save a good deal of time.

USE WHAT YOU HAVE LEARNED

Using the fraction/decimal equivalency chart, fill in the following pay worksheet.

1.

Date	Worker's Name	# Pockets	Fraction	Decimal
8/26/96	6. Marta	42	3/7	.42
	7. Elmer		3/8	
	8. Bill			.44
	9. Susan	56		
	10. Jasmina		8/9	

APPLICATIONS

2. Joan's supervisor asked her to buy .50 yards of material to cover their employee bulletin board. One yard is 36 inches. How many inches of material should she buy?

3. Fred has to deliver a set of documents. His directions are to find Mulberry Street and turn in the driveway $\frac{1}{5}$ mile down the road. When he reaches Mulberry Street, he sets his mileage odometer at 0. What did it read when he arrived at the driveway?

4. Mary was mixing fruit punch for an office party. There are 128 ounces in a gallon. The recipe she was given calls for .50 gallon of orange juice, .25 gallon of pineapple juice, and .25 gallon of coconut milk. How many ounces will this recipe make?

5. Bruce's company car has a ten gallon tank. He gets 30 miles to the gallon. How many miles can he drive on .4 of a tank?

6. Bruce drove 60 miles in the company car. The tank holds 10 gallons, and the car gets 30 miles to the gallon. What decimal part of the tank is used?

7. Fred had to make 100 phone calls this week. By Wednesday he had finished 60. What fraction and decimal of the calls had he completed?

Check your answers on page 99.

LESSON 2   Decimal Place Value and Mixed Decimals

Ruth works in the shipping department of a mail order catalogue warehouse. She weighs and records the weight of each box before it is shipped. Here is a sample of the weights of some boxes she mailed today.

Order #	Contents	Weight
23349	1 set of 6 crystal glasses	3.450 lb.
23350	4 cookbooks	10.543 lb.
23351	2 carved wooden reindeer	4.750 lb.
23352	24 arts and crafts books	62.625 lb.

Decimal Place Value

Whole numbers found to the left of a decimal point have place values and names you probably know, including ones, tens, hundreds, and thousands.

The numbers to the right of a decimal point represent decimal place values and have names, too.

3	4	5	6	.	1	2	3
Thousands	Hundreds	Tens	Ones	Decimal Point	Tenths	Hundreths	Thousandths

Ten**ths**: The first place immediately to the right of the decimal point shows the number of tenths: $\frac{1}{10}$ in the case of the decimal number above.

Hundred**ths**: The second place to the right of the decimal point shows the number of hundredths: $\frac{2}{100}$ in the case of the decimal number above.

Thousand**ths**: The third place to the right of the decimal point shows the number of thousandths: $\frac{3}{1000}$ in the case of the decimal number above.

EXAMPLE 1

Names for decimal numbers

Emma works in the meat department of a grocery store. A new shipment of one-pound steaks has arrived, and her manager has asked her to weigh the individually packaged steaks to check the accuracy of their new supplier. She has to call out the weights for her manager to record.

The weights of the first two steaks are recorded below.

Steak #	Whole Pounds		Tenths of a Pound	Hundredths of a pound	Thousandths of a pound
Steak # 1	1	.	0	0	5
Steak # 2	0	.	9	9	5

Step 1 Look carefully at each place value heading in the example above.

Step 2 Read the first example as, "Steak # 1 weighs one and five thousandths pounds."

Step 3 Read the second example as, "Steak #2 weighs nine hundred ninety-five thousandths pounds."

EXERCISE 2A

Complete Emma's task by writing in the names of these weights.

1.

Steak #	Weight	Use words to write the weight of each steak.
1	1.1	
2	1.05	
3	1.005	
4	0.999	
5	0.955	
6	1.9	
7	1.000	
8	0.855	
9	0.75	
10	0.935	

Check your answers on page 100.

Mixed Decimals

Mixed decimals are numbers with both a whole number and decimal part. For instance, 3.5 is a mixed decimal composed of 3 ones (whole number) and 5 tenths (decimal). The mixed decimal 3.5 is read "three and five tenths."

EXAMPLE 2

$8\frac{1}{2}$ as a mixed number

Sally has been asked to keep track of employee hours by using their time sheets. She must find each employee's hours worked and record the totals in decimal numbers. An example is provided below.

Date	Employee	Time In	Time Out	Hours	Decimal
8/24/96	Smith, J.W.	8:30 a.m.	5:00 p.m.	8 1/2	

Step 1 J.W. Smith worked $8\frac{1}{2}$ hours, that is 8 full hours and one half of another hour. Place the whole eight hours to the left of the decimal in the ones place.

8

Step 2 Use the conversion table on page 1 to find the decimal equivalent for $\frac{1}{2}$.

$$\frac{1}{2} = .5$$

Step 3 Combine these numbers by placing the number of whole hours to the left of the decimal point and the decimal number to the right of the decimal point.

8.5

EXERCISE 2B

Complete the time sheet by recording the hours worked in mixed decimal numbers.

2.

Date	Employee	Time In	Time Out	Hours	Decimal
8/24/96	Smith, J.W.	8:30 a.m.	5:00 p.m.	8 1/2	8.50
	Perez, Al	8:00 a.m.	4:15 p.m.	8 1/4	
	Black, Ann	8:30 a.m.	2:45 p.m.	6 1/4	
	Ortiz, Anna	8:00 a.m.	6:00 p.m.	10	
	Jones, Pat	8:30 a.m.	4:45 p.m.	8 3/4	
	Alto, Eddie	8:15 a.m.	7:00 p.m.	10 3/4	

Check your answers on page 100.

MATH TIP

Notice that the labels of decimal place value all end in "**-ths**" to distinguish them from whole number place value. "Hundreds" refers to whole numbers. "Hundred**ths**" refers to decimals. The word "and" is used to identify the decimal point.

USE WHAT YOU HAVE LEARNED

1. Write each of the five mixed decimals listed below in the correct place in the table.

   a. Mary worked 201.50 hours this month.

   b. John mowed 33.3 acres of lawns this week.

   c. One lady spent $1,020.97 on clothes in our store today.

   d. The largest package in the mailroom today weighed 80.04 pounds.

   e. The gas pump read 10.445 gallons when the tank was full.

Write each decimal number in words.	
	hours
	acres
	dollars
	pounds
	gallons

2. Write the numerical value of the following numbers.

    a. ten dollars and forty-nine cents

    b. five hundred and 5 hundredths

    c. nine hundred ninety-nine thousandths

    d. six tenths

    e. fifty-nine hundredths

3. Circle any decimal numbers that have a 0 in the tenths place.

    a. 1.300   **b.** 0.005   **c.** 0.094   **d.** 4.505   **e.** 8.099

4. Circle any decimal numbers that have a 0 in the hundredths place.

    a. 4.303   **b.** 0.005   **c.** 0.094   **d.** 4.055   **e.** 8.099

5. Circle any decimal numbers that have a 0 in the thousandths place.

    a. 6.503   **b.** 0.005   **c.** 9.990   **d.** 4.050   **e.** 8.110

APPLICATIONS

6. Jack has $5.25 in the company's petty cash account. He has to mail a package which will cost 5 and $\frac{1}{2}$ dollars. Does he have enough money to mail the package?

7. Jane's package weighs 4.825 pounds. Express this weight in words.

8. Fred is working as an administrative assistant in an office. He must buy one box of staples at $0.99; one pen at $1.00; one ream of paper at $3.95; one pencil sharpener at $10.98; and one file cabinet at $39.95. Code each number in the following list as W = Whole number, D = Decimal number, or M = Mixed Decimal.

9. At the annual company picnic, .2 of the production employees were awarded certificates and pins for perfect attendance. Express this decimal fraction in words.

Fred's Shopping List		
Catalog Item	Price	W/M/D
Staples	$ 0.99	
Pens	$ 1.00	
Paper	$ 3.95	
Pencil Sharpener	$ 10.98	
File Cabinet	$ 39.95	

Check your answers
on page 101

LESSON 3 Converting Decimals to Fractions

Frank writes advertising copy, converting statistics into simple, everyday language. He reads that .75 of 1,000 people surveyed prefer his company's glass cleaner. He must convert the decimal to a simple fraction in order to rewrite this information in a simple way.

Converting Decimals to Fractions

Decimals can be expressed as fractions whose denominators are multiples of 10. Three tenths, .3, equals $\frac{3}{10}$. Forty-two hundredths, .42, equals $\frac{42}{100}$. Six hundred forty-one thousandths, .641, equals $\frac{641}{1000}$.

EXAMPLE 1

Convert .75 into a fraction

Step 1	Place the decimal without the decimal point in the numerator position.	75
Step 2	Count the number of decimal places to the right of the decimal point. The two places to the right of the decimal point tell you that the decimal is expressed as hundredths. Use 100 as the denominator.	$\frac{75}{100}$
Step 3	Simplify this fraction to its lowest terms.	$\frac{75}{100} = \frac{3}{4}$

Become familiar with the names of decimal places. If you are still a little uncertain, refer to the chart reproduced here.

3	4	5	6	.	1	2	3
Thousands	Hundreds	Tens	Ones	Decimal Point	Tenths	Hundreths	Thousandths

EXERCISE 3A

Convert the following one-digit decimals to fractions.

1. .3 **2.** .5 **3.** .1 **4.** .6 **5.** .8

Convert the following two-digit decimals to fractions.

6. .25   **7.** .33   **8.** .57   **9.** .70   **10.** .75

APPLICATION

Check your answers on page 101.

11. Thirty-five hundredths of the 500 employees in Jon's company have not taken any sick leave this year. What fraction have taken no leave?

Converting Mixed Decimals to Fractions

Mixed decimals have the whole number to the left of the decimal point. Mixed numbers are made up of a whole number and a fraction. The steps to convert mixed decimals to mixed numbers are the same as those above with one more step. Here is how to convert 3.125 to a mixed number.

EXAMPLE 2

Convert 3.125 to a mixed number

Step 1	Place the whole number to the left of the fraction you are going to create.	$3\frac{}{}$
Step 2	Place the decimal number (values to the right of the decimal point) in the numerator position. Omit the decimal point.	$3\frac{125}{}$
Step 3	Count the number of decimal places to the right of the decimal point. The three places to the right of the decimal point tell you that the decimal is expressed as thousandths. Use 1,000 as the denominator.	$3\frac{125}{1000}$
Step 4	Simplify the fraction to its lowest terms.	$3\frac{1}{8}$

EXERCISE 3B

Convert the following mixed decimals into mixed numbers.

12. 5.35   **13.** 7.500   **14.** 4.125   **15.** 5.666   **16.** 9.8

APPLICATION

Check your answers on page 102.

17. Jim was sent to the hardware store to buy 6.25 pounds of nails. The scale is calibrated in fractions. Convert this mixed decimal to a mixed number.

MATH
TIP

Counting the number of places to the right of the decimal point indicates how many zeros will appear on the right of the number 1 in the denominator.

$$.234 = \frac{234}{1000}$$

3 places   3 0s

USE WHAT YOU HAVE LEARNED

Convert the following three-digit decimal numbers to simple fractions.

1. .125   **2.** .875   **3.** .500   **4.** .250

APPLICATIONS

5. Four tenths of the employees in Jon's company were given raises at the end of the year. What fraction got raises?

6. When Bill orders office supplies from an out-of-state mail-order supplier, he saves .08 in sales tax. Express .08 as a fraction.

7. Women are .48 of the total employees. What fraction of the employees are women?

8. Frank is writing a press release about his company's newest product. Of those surveyed, .875 gave it an A+ rating. Express this as a fraction.

9. Marie has reached seventy-five hundredths of her sales quota. What fractional part of her quota has she met?

10. Ester has worked 10.25 hours today. She is paid $8.00 per hour. Convert her hours to a fraction and multiply by 8 to find out her daily wages.

Check your answers on page 102.

LESSON 4 Metric Units

Ernesto, who works for an import/export company, must be familiar with terms such as meters, liters, and grams because most of the imports he deals with are measured in the Metric System.

The Metric System is a system of measurement that is easily expressed in decimals. Some people think it is simple and easy to work with. This lesson is an introduction to meters, liters, and grams.

Meters

A *meter* (about 39 inches, 3.25 feet) is a measure of linear length that is a little longer than 1 yard (36 inches, 3 feet). Here is a chart that shows metric length.

EXAMPLE 1

A meter is how many centimeters?

Equivalency Chart

Place Value	Numerical Value	Metric System	Metric System Building Blocks	English System
Whole Numbers				
thousands	1,000.000	kilometer	=10 hectometers	1 mile=1.6 km
hundreds	100.000	hectometer	=10 decameters	
tens	10.000	decameter	=10 meters	
units	1.000	meter	=10 decimeters	1 yard=.9 meter
Decimal Numbers				
tenths	.100	decimeter	=10 centimeters	
hundredths	.010	centimeter	=10 millimeters	2.54 cm=1 inch
thousandths	.001	millimeter		

Use the chart above to help you find how many centimeters are in one meter.

Step 1 Locate meters and centimeters on the chart.

Step 2 A meter is made up of 10 decimeters. Each decimeter is a group of 10 centimeters. So, a meter is 10 groups of 10 centimeters.

Step 3 One meter = 10 × 10 centimeters = 100 centimeters. One meter equals 100 centimeters.

EXERCISE 4A

Circle the correct answer inside the parentheses. < means *is less than*, > means *is greater than*

1. one mile (<, is the same as, >) one kilometer

2. one inch (<, is the same as, >) one centimeter

3. one hectometer (< , is the same as, >) one kilometer

4. one millimeter (< , is the same as, >) one centimeter

APPLICATION

Check your answers
on page 102.

5. Bert needs to buy a new 14-guage extension cord for his shop. He
finds 2 different cords that cost $16.29. Cord A is 50 feet. Cord B is
18 meters. Which cord is longer?

Liters

A *liter* (about 1.06 quarts) is a measure of liquid volume that is a
little more than 1 quart (32 ounces). Here is a chart that shows
metric volume.

EXAMPLE 2

A liter is how many milliliters?

Equivalency Chart

Place Value	Numerical Value	Metric System	Metric System Building Blocks	English System
Whole Numbers				
thousands	1,000.000	kiloliter	=10 hectoliters	
hundreds	100.000	hectoliter	=10 decaliters	
tens	10.000	decaliter	=10 liters	
units	1.000	liter	=10 deciliters	1 liter = 1.06 qt.
Decimal Numbers				1 quart=.95 liter
tenths	.100	deciliter	=10 centiliters	
hundredths	.010	centiliter	=10 milliliters	
thousandths	.001	milliliter		1 ounce =30 ml

Use the chart above to help you find how many milliliters are in one
liter.

Step 1 Locate liters and milliliters on the chart.

Step 2 A liter is made up of 10 deciliters. Each deciliter is a group
of 10 centiliters. Each centiliter is a group of 10 milliliters.
So, a liter is 10 groups of 10 groups of 10 milliliters.

Step 3 One liter = 10 × 10 × 10 milliliters = 1,000 milliliters. One
liter = 1,000 milliliters

EXERCISE 4B

**Circle the correct answer inside the parentheses. < means *is less than*,
> means *is greater than***

6. one liter is (< , is the same as, >) one quart

7. one deciliter is (< , is the same as, >) ten centiliters

8. one hectoliter is (<,   is the same as,   >   ) one hundred liters

9. one deciliter is (<,   is the same as,   >   ) one hundred milliliters

APPLICATION

Check your answers on page 103.

10. Stephanie needs to buy 50-weight tractor oil. Two different brands cost $10.68 per case. Case A contains 12 1-quart bottles. Case B contains 12 1-liter bottles. Which case contains more oil?

Grams

A *gram* (28 grams = one ounce, 1 kilogram = 2.2 pounds) is a measure of weight. Here is a chart that shows the metric weight.

EXAMPLE 3

A gram is how many milligrams?

Equivalency Chart

Place Value	Numerical Value	Metric System	Metric System Building Blocks	English System
Whole Numbers				
thousands	1,000.000	kilogram	=10 hectograms	1 kg. = 2.2 lb.
hundreds	100.000	hectogram	=10 decagrams	
tens	10.000	decagram	=10 grams	
units	1.000	gram	=10 decigrams	454 gm. = 1 lb.
Decimal Numbers				
tenths	.100	decigram	=10 centigrams	
hundredths	.010	centigram	=10 milligrams	
thousandths	.001	milligram		

Use the chart above to help you find how many milligrams are in one gram.

Step 1   Locate grams and milligrams on the chart.

Step 2   A gram is made up of 10 decigrams. Each decigram is group of 10 centigrams. Each centigram is group of 10 milligrams. So, a gram is 10 groups of 10 groups of milligrams.

Step 3   One gram = $10 \times 10 \times 10$ milligrams = 1,000 milligrams. One gram = 1,000 milligrams

EXERCISE 4C

Circle the correct answer inside the parenthesis. < means *is less than*, > means *is greater than*

11. one kilogram is (<,   is the same as,   >   ) one pound

12. .5 a gram is (<,   is the same as,   >   ) 500 decigrams

13. one kilogram is (<, is the same as, >) one thousand grams

14. one decagram (<, is the same as, >) ten grams

APPLICATION

Check your answers
on page 103.

15. Juana is buying flour for her bakery. Supplier A offers to sell her 100 pounds of flour for $89.00. Supplier B will sell her 100 kilograms for the same price. Which supplier is cheaper?

USE WHAT YOU HAVE LEARNED

Use the equivalency charts to help you answer these questions.

1. How many millimeters are in a meter?

2. How many centiliters are in a liter?

3. How many decigrams are in a kilogram?

APPLICATIONS

4. John works in the dry goods section of a wholesale warehouse. A customer wants to buy one pound of cayenne spice. This spice is imported in 50 mg packets. About how many packets does he need to make-up the one pound order for this customer?

5. Mark sews. The pattern he must use calls for 3 meters of material. Is this more than or less than 3 yards?

6. Aldo is a server. He serves juice in 4 ounce servings. How many milliliters are in one serving?

7. Roberto has a choice between loading 1,000 pounds of fruit onto one truck or loading 1,000 grams of fruit onto another truck. Which task should be easier?

8. Leon works on the loading dock, moving bags of rice that weigh 4,540 gm per bag. He can lift 100 pounds at a time. How many sacks of rice can he move at one time?

9. Mike is installing environmentally beneficial water filters. The expected life span of each filter is 10,000 kiloliters. How many liters of water can one filter process?

Check your answers
on page 103.

LESSON 5 Rounding Decimals

Nancy works in a retail store selling clothes. Because the sales tax in her city is .076, her calculator often returns an answer with three decimal places. In these cases, she must round the answer to two decimal places, so that the total can be expressed in dollars and cents.

The procedure for rounding decimals is similar to rounding whole numbers. If the number to the right of the given place is 4 or less, then drop it and any other numbers to its right. If the number to the right of the given place is greater than 4, then raise the given place by one and drop all numbers to the right.

EXAMPLE 1

Round 4.33 and 6.85 to the nearest whole number.

Step 1	Locate the ones place.	4. 33 6.85
Step 2	If the number to the right of the ones place is 4 or less, then drop it and any other numbers to its right.	4.33 = 4.33 = 4 4
Step 3	If the number to the right of the ones place is greater than 4, then raise the ones place by 1 and drop any other numbers to its right.	6.85 = (6.85 + 1) = 7 7

EXERCISE 5A

Round the following decimals to the nearest whole number.

1. 1.6   **2.** 2.99   **3.** 6.2   **4.** 8.333   **5.** 5.50

APPLICATION

6. Jack works in a lumber yard. He has been asked to count cords of lumber. Several cords have been opened in order to sell single pieces of lumber. He has been asked to count the number of full cords and round off the opened cords to full units. After his inventory he finds 10.5 cords of $2 \times 4 \times 8$ ft., 15.3 cords of $2 \times 4 \times 10$ ft., and 12.9 cords of $2 \times 4 \times 12$ ft. How many cords does he have in total?

Check your answers on page 104.

Rounding Decimals to the Nearest Tenth

To round decimals to the nearest tenth, evaluate the value in the hundredths place.

EXAMPLE 2

Round 4.532 and 6.585 to the nearest tenth.

Step 1	Locate the tenths place.	4.532 6.585
Step 2	If the number to the right of the tenths place is 4 or less, then drop it and any numbers to its right.	4.532 = 4.532 = 4.5 4.5
Step 3	If the number to the right of the tenths place is greater than 4, raise the tenths place by 1 and drop any numbers to its right.	6.585 = (6.585 + .1) = 6.6 6.6

EXERCISE 5B

Round the following decimals to the nearest tenth.

7. 1.563   **8.** 2.590   **9.** 6.22   **10.** 8.435   **11.** 5.55

APPLICATION

12. Mark, an apprentice plumber, is counting PVC pipe for a new job. This type of pipe is purchased in 100 piece lots. He finds 2.36 lots of 1 inch pipe and 1.49 lots of 1.5 inch pipe. How many lots of each type of pipe, rounded to the nearest tenth, does he have?

Check your answers on page 104.

Rounding Decimals to the Nearest Hundredth

To round decimals to the nearest hundredth, evaluate the value in the thousandths place.

EXAMPLE 3

Round 4.5532 and 6.558 to the nearest hundredth.

Step 1	Locate the hundredths place.	4.5532 6.558
Step 2	If the number to the right of the hundredths place is 4 or less, then drop it and any others found to its right.	4.5532 = 4.5532 = 4.55 4.55
Step 3	If the number to the right of the hundredths place is greater than 4, then raise the hundredths place by 1 and drop the numbers to its right.	6.558 = (6.558 + .01) = 6.56 6.56

EXERCISE 5C

Round the following decimals to the nearest hundredth.

13. 7.777   **14.** 9.432   **15.** 4.567   **16.** 5.555   **17.** 1.123

APPLICATION

18. The price of orders in Helen's company, including shipping and handling, is automatically calculated in mixed decimals to the thousandth place. She must round these to the nearest hundredth in order to bill customers. How much should she bill for the following orders?

Check your answers on page 104.

Date	Order #	Computed Cost	Price
9/25/95	00123	14.255	$
	00124	18.749	$
	00125	39.3333	$

Keep it simple. Focus on the given place and the place immediately to its right.

USE WHAT YOU HAVE LEARNED

Complete the following chart by rounding the numbers to the nearest hundredth, tenth, or whole number.

1.

Decimal number	Round to hundredths	Round to tenths	Round to ones
10.549			
25.089			
1.493			
9.769			
33.333			

APPLICATIONS

2. Aikiko, who works in a fabric store, has 10.55 meters of blue silk, 5.79 meters of red silk, and 32.00 meters of yellow silk. This fabric is sold for $1.20 for one tenth of a yard. Convert her inventory into mixed decimals rounded to the nearest tenth.

3. Allan drove his delivery truck 39.255 miles. What was his mileage rounded to the nearest hundredth?

4. The cost of a package including shipping and handling is 34.667 dollars. Rewrite this in dollars and cents.

5. After figuring in her discount, the cost of a new computer for Anna's office is $2,005.335. How much, in dollars and cents, should she write on the company check to pay for this item?

6. Sal must weigh shipments of catalogue ordered goods and record their weight rounded to the nearest tenth next to their order number. Complete the rounding column in his worksheet.

Date	Order #	Weight	Wt. rounded
9/25/95	00123	12.33 lb.	
	00124	18.64 lb.	
	00125	29.37 lb.	

7. Bill is planning a big project. He will need to have at least 12 boxes (10 discs each) of 2HD computer discs. After checking the supply room, he finds 53 discs. How many full boxes are on hand and how many will he have to buy?

Check your answers on page 105.

LESSON 6   Comparing Decimals

Alejandro must find a suitable piece of real estate for a client who wants to build a new office building on a site with a minimum of 2.35 acres. Which of the following pieces of land are suitable?

Lot 23 2.555 acres
Lot 49 1.89 acres
Lot 64 2.3 acres

Comparing Decimals

In order to compare decimals, first add zeros where necessary to give each decimal number the same number of decimal places. Zeros can be added on to the right of the last decimal place without changing the value of the number.

EXAMPLE 1

Compare 2.555, 1.89, and 2.3. Which are greater than 2.35?

Step 1   Make sure all decimal values to be compared have the same number of decimal places.

Lot 23 already has three decimal places, so nothing needs be added.   **2.555**

Lot 49 has two decimal places. Add one decimal place by adding a zero in the thousandths place.   **1.89**0

Lot 64 has one decimal place. Add two decimal places by adding one zero in the hundredths place and another zero in the thousandths place.   **2.3**00

The client's minimum lot size is 2.35 acres. This number has only two decimal places, so a zero must be added in the thousandths place.   **2.35**0

Step 2   First compare the whole numbers in each lot to the whole number in the minimum lot size required.

In Lot 23 the whole number in 2.555 is equal to the 2 in 2.350.

In Lot 49 the whole number in 1.890 is less than the 2 in 2.350.

Therefore Lot 49 is not suitable.

In Lot 64 the whole number in 2.300 is equal to the 2 in 2.350

Step 3   Compare the tenths place value of the possible numbers to the minimum size requirement of 2.350.

In Lot 23 2.555 and 2.350   .5 > .3

In Lot 64 2.**3**00 and 2.**3**50   .3 is equal to .3

Therefore both lots are suitable at this level.

Step 4   Compare the hundredths place value of the possible numbers to the minimum size requirement of 2.350.

In Lot 23 2.5**5**5 and 2.3**5**0   .05 is equal to .05

In Lot 64 2.3**0**0 and 2.3**5**0   .00 < .05

Therefore, Lot 64 is not suitable.

Step 5   Compare the thousandths place value of the possible numbers to the minimum size requirement of 2.350.

In Lot 23   2.555 > 2.350

This is the only suitable lot.

EXERCISE 6

Compare the decimal numbers in Column A to the decimal numbers in Column C at the tenth place value. Insert the appropriate sign, < , ⊃ or = in Column B.

	A	B	C
1.	1.5	____	2.5
2.	1.55	____	1.6
3.	3.49	____	3.44
4.	7.84	____	7.85
5.	0.19	____	0.20

APPLICATION

6. Frank receives two packages. One weighs 32.75 lb., and the other weighs 32.8 lb. Which package is heavier?

Check your answers on page 106.

MATH TIP   Adding zeros to the end of decimals does not change their values. Understanding how to use zeros to even columns will be an important help when adding and subtracting decimals.

USE WHAT YOU HAVE LEARNED

Compare the decimal numbers in Column A to the decimal numbers in Column C at the hundredth place value. Insert the appropriate sign (<, > or =) in Column B.

	A	B	C		A	B	C		A	B	C
1.	9.364	——	9.367	2.	5.252	——	5.255	3.	8.234	——	8.235
4.	1.115	——	1.119	5.	3.353	——	3.354				

APPLICATION

6. The hardware store where Salvatore works is having a sale on nails in one pound bags. Sal must weigh five bags on a digital scale. Those bags with less than .995 of a pound will need more nails. Compare the decimal weights to the standard and place a check mark next to those that need more nails.

   Bag #1 = 0.870   Bag #2 = 0.995

   Bag #3 = 0.750   Bag #4 = 0.969

   Bag #5 = 0.999

7. Joan must find a suitable piece of real estate for a client who wants to build a home on a site with a minimum lot size of 1.5 acres. Which of the following pieces of land are at least that size?

   Lot 25 1.555 acres

   Lot 48 1.899 acres

   Lot 65 1.479 acres

8. Anna has 3.75 meters of material left over. Which pattern can she make?

   Pattern A 3.78 meters

   Pattern B 3.72 meters

   Pattern C 3.77 meters

9. John's truck gets 30 miles to the gallon. He has 3 gallons left. Which destination can he reach safely?

   Destination A 90.5 miles

   Destination B 85.333 miles

10. Three postal workers walked 2.47 miles, 3.352 miles, and 3.355 miles. Which one walked the farthest distance?

11. Packages weighing between 2.00 and 2.50 lb. can be sent at a less expensive rate. Which of the following packages qualify?

    Package A 2.444 lb.

    Package B 2.499 lb.

    Package C 2.555 lb.

Check your answers
on page 106.

CHAPTER 1 Summary

Decimal Fractions

A decimal is a number with a decimal point in it. It is another way to show a fraction or a part of something. Like a fraction, a decimal can show a value less than one.

Look at the chart of fractional equivalency reproduced below.

Fraction/Decimal Equivalency Chart

# Pockets	Fraction	Decimal	# Pockets	Fraction	Decimal	# Pockets	Fraction	Decimal
50	1/2	.50	17	1/6	.17	38	3/8	.38
33	1/3	.33	83	5/6	.83	63	5/8	.63
66	2/3	.66	14	1/7	.14	88	7/8	.88
25	1/4	.25	28	2/7	.28	11	1/9	.11
75	3/4	.75	42	3/7	.42	22	2/9	.22
20	1/5	.20	57	4/7	.57	44	4/9	.44
40	2/5	.40	71	5/7	.71	56	5/9	.56
60	3/5	.60	86	6/7	.86	78	7/9	.78
80	4/5	.80	13	1/8	.13	89	8/9	.89

Decimal Place Value

Decimal place value is similar to the place value system you learned for whole numbers. The name for the places are indicated to the right of the decimal point in the graphic below.

3	4	5	6	.	1	2	3
Thousands	Hundreds	Tens	Ones	Decimal Point	Tenths	Hundreths	Thousandths

EXERCISE A

1. Circle any number that has zero in the hundredths place.

3,013.4   701.407   32.086   9.409

2. Circle any number that has zero in the tenths place.

Check your answers on page 107.

3,300.4   401.007   54.021   6.109

Writing Decimal Fractions in Words

When writing decimal fractions in words, the word "and" is used to signify the position of the decimal point. Place value labels end in "-ths": tenths, hundredths, thousandths.

EXERCISE B

Write the following decimal fractions in words.

3. .034

4. 42.28

Supply the decimal fraction for each of the following.

5. Three hundred twenty-six and three tenths

Check your answers on page 107.

6. Two hundred and three hundredths

Converting Decimals to Fractions.

You convert decimals into fractions by using the decimal (without the decimal point) as a numerator and the appropriate multiple of 10 as the denominator. If the decimal contains 3 decimal places, use 1 followed by 3 zeros for a denominator. Reduce the resulting fraction to its lowest terms.

EXERCISE C

Check your answers on page 107.

Convert the following decimals to fractions.

7. .67 =   8. .4 =   9. .425 =

Rounding Decimals

It is sometimes helpful to round off decimals. Money is usually rounded to the nearest hundredth.

Round the following numbers to the nearest tenth.

10. .76   **11.** .44   **12.** .426

Round the following numbers to the nearest hundredth.

Check your answers
on page 107.

13. .264   **14.** 0.694   **15.** .7618

Comparing Decimals

A reliable way to compare decimals is to be sure that each decimal has the same number of decimal places. If one decimal has more places than another, then add zeros to the decimal with fewer places.

EXERCISE E

Circle the smaller decimal in each pair.

Check your answers
on page 107.

16. .16   .1569   **17.** .6   .4999   **18.** .3376   .33

MATH AT WORK

1. **Cashier**   Daphne is a cashier. She makes $12 an hour when she works overtime at Mastrini's Grocery. How much will she make if she works .75 hours of overtime?

2. **Delivery**   Driver Fred has to deliver a dish washer. He has been instructed to turn north on Mary Street and turn in the driveway 1/2 mile down the road on the right. When he reaches Mary Street, he sets his mileage odometer at 0. What should it read when he arrives at the driveway?

3. **Delivery Driver**   Mary is a courier. Her motorcycle ran out of gas. Her tank holds two gallons or 64 ounces. She has three containers which hold .5 gallons, .25 gallons, and .25 gallons. What decimal part of her tank will these three containers fill?

4. **Salesperson**   Barry is making a 300 mile drive to a sales meeting. He has driven 210 miles. What part of the trip has he completed? Express the answer as a decimal.

5. **Salesperson**   Barry drove 180 miles in the company car. The tank holds 10 gallons and the car gets 30 miles to the gallon. What decimal part of the tank is left?

6. **Plumber**   Doris is installing a water filtration system. There are three sizes of tube included with the kit: .28 inch, .255 inch, and .095 inch. Which tube is the largest?

7. Boatwright David is repairing the hull in a fiberglass boat. The cracked area is 12 inches by 46 inches. David buys rolls of fiberglass lattice that are 50 cm wide. He has 2 meters left. Does he have enough lattice to cover the cracked area with one solid piece?

8. Horticulturist Darnell buys 4 yards of bird netting to protect some new plantings. Is this more than or less than 4 meters of netting?

9. Nurse Doreen is a nurse. Her patient is receiving glucose solution at the rate of 20 centiliters per hour. At this rate, how many hours will it take for the patient to receive 1 liter of solution?

10. Nurse When Doreen assists in the delivery room, she watches the fetal monitors closely. She can time the mother's contractions based on the peaks recorded on the paper tape produced by the machine. The tape moves at 1 meter per hour. If the peaks recorded are 10 centimeters apart, how much time has passed between them?

11. Mechanic When Mike does an oil change, he removes an average of 3.75 liters of oil from a vehicle. He has a 500 liter waste-oil disposal tank. About how many oil changes can he do before he fills his disposal tank? Round your answer to the nearest whole number.

12. Bookkeeper Molly is a bookkeeper. As she is recording payments, she comes to a check that is written for two thousand, seven hundred forty-seven and twenty-three hundredths dollars. What number should Molly enter?

13. Delivery Driver Allan drove his delivery truck 39.255 miles. What was his mileage rounded to the nearest hundredth?

14. Secretary The cost of a new printer for Anna's computer is 1,003.935 dollars. How much, in dollars and cents, should she write on the company check to pay for this item?

15. Plumber Alex's work load today calls for laying 1.55 meters, 2.66 meters, and 3.75 meters of PVC pipe. How many whole meters of pipe will he need?

16. Retail Clerk The hardware store where Salvatore works is having a sale on ten penny nails in one pound bags. Sal must spot check five bags on a digital scale. Those bags with less than .95 lb. must be removed. How many of the following bags must be removed?

Bag #1 = 0.877   Bag #2 = 0.945

Bag #3 = 0.950   Bag #4 = 0.949

Bag #5 = 0.955

17. Real Estate Broker Joanne's client wants her to buy a parcel of land between 1 and 1.5 acres to build a home. Which of the following parcels of land should she consider?

Lot 25 1.455 acres

Lot 48 1.859 acres

Lot 65 1.479 acres

18. Garment Worker Anna has 3.66 meters of material left over. Which pattern can she make?

Pattern A $3\frac{3}{4}$ meters

Pattern B $3\frac{2}{3}$ meters

Pattern C 3.76 meters

MATH AT WORK

19. Delivery Driver John's truck gets 21 miles to the gallon. He has 3 gallons left. Which destination can he reach safely?

Destination A 50.5 miles

Destination B 65.333 miles

20. Shipping Clerk Packages weighing under 2.750 lb. can be sent at a less expensive rate. Which of the following packages qualify?

Package A 2.744 lb.

Package B 2.799 lb.

Package C 2.755 lb.

21. Secretary Shelly is shopping for office supplies. She finds reams of white office paper (8.5" × 11") for three different prices. Which is the best price?

a. two dollars and nine hundred fifty thousandths

b. two dollars and eighty-nine hundredths

c. two dollars and ninety-five thousandths

22. Telephone Technician Chris, a telephone installer, turned in a time sheet for 5 jobs completed on Monday. He worked .5 hr., .35 hr., .75 hr., .66 hr. and .87 hr.. He bills customers $30 for the first half hour and $20 for the second half hour or any part thereof. How much money did Chris bring in on Monday?

23. Line Worker Pat works on an assembly line making widgets. He is paid $50 per gross (144). His production for one week was: Mon =.979 gross, Tue = .898 gross, Wed = .995 gross, Thu = .985 gross, Fri = .997 gross. Which day did he make the most money?

24. Shipping Clerk Yolanda, a shipping clerk was asked to monitor outgoing packages from three salespersons for one week and report the highest producer. The weekly totals were as follows:

Salesperson #1 shipped a total of 495.335 lb.

Salesperson #2 shipped a total of 495.536 lb.

Salesperson #3 shipped a total of 495.455 lb.

Which salesperson shipped the largest total?

Check your answers on page 107.

CHAPTER 2

Adding and Subtracting Decimals

LESSON 7   Adding Decimals

Fran is buying two adjacent tracts of land to start a camp for children. One has 9.8 acres and the other has 6.4 acres. Fran adds the numbers together to find the total number of acres she is going to buy.

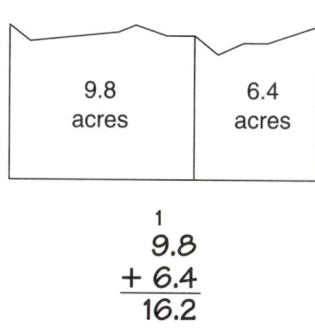

Adding Tenths

The illustration at right shows how Fran solved the problem to find the total number of acres she will buy. This procedure is the same as adding whole numbers, but the decimal points must be in a straight column.

$$\begin{array}{r} \overset{1}{}9.8 \\ +\ 6.4 \\ \hline 16.2 \end{array}$$

EXAMPLE 1

80.6 + 56.9 = ?

The land Fran is buying has 80.6 feet and 56.9 feet of property along the lake. How many feet of lakefront property is Fran buying?

$$
\begin{array}{cccc}
\begin{array}{r} . \\ + \ . \\ \hline . \end{array} &
\begin{array}{r} 80.6 \\ +56.9 \\ \hline . \end{array} &
\begin{array}{r} \overset{1}{}80.6 \\ +56.9 \\ \hline .5 \end{array} &
\begin{array}{r} \overset{1\ \ 1}{}80.6 \\ +56.9 \\ \hline 137.5 \end{array} \\
\text{Step 1} & \text{Step 2} & \text{Step 3} & \text{Step 4}
\end{array}
$$

Step 1 Fran writes the problem vertically. She writes a decimal point for each number in a column. She is careful to line up the decimal points. She also writes another decimal point under the others in the answer space. She writes the addition sign.

Step 2 Fran writes the numbers with decimal points. She writes the tenths to the right of the decimal point and the whole numbers to the left.

Step 3 Fran adds the numbers just as she would add whole numbers. She starts with the column on the right. Fran first adds the tenths: 6 + 9 = 15. She writes the 5 in the tenths column and regroups the new 1. She writes a 1 above the ones column.

Step 4 Then Fran adds the ones: 1 + 0 + 6 = 7. Fran adds the tens: 8 + 5 = 13. She writes the 3 in the tens column. She regroups the 1 hundred and adds the hundreds column: 1 + 0 + 0 = 1. Fran writes the 1 in the hundreds column.

EXERCISE 7A

Write the numbers in columns. Then add.

1. 2.4 + 5.3 = ?

2. 18.7 + 11.9 = ?

3. 42.5 + 28.6 = ?

4. 23.9 + 10.4 = ?

APPLICATION

Check your answers on page 111.

5. Fran wants to know how far the camp will be from town. She drives 26.2 miles on the highway and 11.9 miles to the gate. How far is the camp from town?

Adding Hundredths

To add numbers that have a hundredths column, follow the same procedure for adding decimals, but start by adding the hundredths column first.

EXAMPLE 2

54.98 + 27.06 = ?

Step 1 Write the problem vertically. Write the decimal points for the numbers and the answer in a straight line. Write the addition sign.

$$\begin{array}{r} . \\ +\ . \\ \hline . \end{array}$$

Step 2 Write the numbers with the decimal points.

$$\begin{array}{r} 54.98 \\ +27.06 \\ \hline . \end{array}$$

Step 3 Add the hundredths column. Add the tenths column. Add the ones column. Add the tens column. Regroup when you need to.

$$\begin{array}{r} {}^{1\ 1\ 1} \\ 54.98 \\ +27.06 \\ \hline 82.04 \end{array}$$

EXERCISE 7B

Write the numbers in columns. Then add.

6. 5.22 + 1.74 = ?

7. 33.08 + 18.73 = ?

8. 56.49 + 30.96 = ?

9. 295.35 + 162.28 = ?

APPLICATION

Check your answers on page 111.

10. Sarah prepares the bills for the Clark Disposal Company. The company charges $9.50 for garbage and recycling services and a sales tax of $2.47. What is the total amount of the bill?

MATH TIP To add three or more decimal numbers, write the numbers in a column. Keep the decimals in a straight line. Then add each column of numbers.

USE WHAT YOU HAVE LEARNED

Write the numbers in columns. Then add.

1. 8.4 + 6.3 = ?

2. 93.57 + 41.23 = ?

3. 28.62 + 19.08 + 15.75 = ?

APPLICATIONS

4. Ted pumps 3.5 gallons of gas into his car and 2.5 gallons into a gas can. How many gallons of gas does Ted pump?

5. Shawna works for the weather service tracking the rain the city gets. For the first three months of the year, she records 6.3 inches, 2.8 inches, and 7.4 inches of rain. According to Shawna's records, how much rain did the city get?

6. Ernie is building a fence on two sides of a building. One side will be 17.33 meters long and the other 23.69 meters. What is the total length of the fence?

7. Nancy is a jewelry designer. A customer gives her three pieces of gold jewelry to smelt and form into a new necklace. The pieces weigh .98, .23, and .76 ounces. How many ounces of gold does Nancy have for the new necklace?

8. Patty sells a pool that is 16.5 meters long by 8.3 meters wide. The customer decides to include a Jacuzzi. Patty needs to add another 2.7 meters to the width of the pool. What will be the width of that part of the pool?

9. Carlos orders business cards that cost $23.95 and stationary with the company name that cost $47.86. How much does Carlos pay before sales tax is added?

Check your answers
on page 111.

LESSON 8   Adding Decimals with Different Place Values

Thasha is a draftsman. She is working on a full scale schematic for a new stereo receiver. A wire that connects four components is represented on the diagram by a straight line. It is two and three tenths centimeters from the first connection to the second connection, four centimeters from the second to the third connection, and eighty-eight hundredths of a centimeter from the third to the fourth connection. Thasha needs to find out the overall length of the wire.

Adding Decimal Fractions

The technique you know for lining up decimal points is useful when you are computing decimals with different place values.

EXAMPLE 1

Look at Thasha's problem.

$$
\begin{array}{cccc}
. & 2.3 & 2.30 & \overset{1}{2.30} \\
. & 4. & 4.00 & 4.00 \\
\underline{+\;.} & \underline{+\;.88} & \underline{+\;.88} & \underline{+\;.88} \\
. & . & . & 7.18 \\
\text{Step 2} & \text{Step 3} & \text{Step 4} & \text{Step 5}
\end{array}
$$

Step 1 Thasha counts the number of items she needs to add. There are three.

Step 2 Thasha then creates a column of three decimal points. She draws the addition bar, and then places a decimal point underneath the bar in the same column for the answer.

Step 3 She writes the numbers with decimal points. Remember, the word "and" usually signals the position of the decimal point.

Step 4 To help her keep the columns aligned, Thasha adds zeros to the decimals. Remember, these zeros do not change the value of the numbers.

Step 5 Then she adds.

EXERCISE 8

Convert the following into vertical columns and add.

1. $2.3 + 26 + .003 =$ **2.** $6 + .6 + .0006 =$

3. .014 + 7.6 + 11 =

4. .003 + .3 + 237 =

APPLICATION

Check your answers
on page 112.

5. Every day at 2:00 p.m., Mary leaves work and drives two and four tenths miles from her office to the express mail office. Then she drives an additional three miles to the post office. It is four and four tenths miles from the post office back to her office. How many miles can she claim for each day's trip?

It is worthwhile to check to be sure the numbers are aligned properly before you add.

USE WHAT YOU HAVE LEARNED

Convert the following into vertical columns and add.

1. .3 + 2.6 + .009 =

2. 6.3 + 19 + 142 =

3. .1 + 9.452 + 2 =

4. .005 + .023 + 421 =

5. 16 + .01 + .003 =

6. 3 + 5 + .0006 =

7. .023 + 5.4 + 21=

8. .034 + .6 + 10 =

9. Darlene is in charge of timing chemical reactions in the lab. The first reaction takes 2.3 seconds, the second reaction takes 1.85 seconds, and the third takes .47 seconds. What is the total time of the three reactions?

10. Bill purchases a new hammer for $16.89, a bottle of chalk for $1.39, and a package of scraper blades for $ .89. What was the total amount of his purchase?

11. Doris works for the Department of Fish and Wildlife. She studies beach pollution. In one week, she collected eleven and twenty-two hundredths pounds of plastic refuse at one site, six pounds at another, and three and two tenths pounds at the third. What was the total weight of plastic refuse collected for the week?

12. Tom is planning a trip to meet with some suppliers. His flight to San Antonio takes two hours. Then it takes about 1.25 hours to drive from San Antonio to Austin. How long will his trip take?

13. Juan needs to express mail a package. He wants to use a letter-sized mailing envelope, but there is an eight-ounce weight limit. He needs to mail a twenty-page report weighing four and thirty-four thousandths ounces and a photograph weighing eight tenths of an ounce. The mailing envelope itself weighs one and a half ounces. What is the total weight of Juan's package?

14. When Doris started with the Fish and Wildlife Department, she worked in a fish hatchery. Six months after their release, Doris received word that three of the fish had been caught. The three fishes' weights were reported as fourteen and twenty-eight hundredths ounces, eleven and two tenths ounces, and thirteen ounces. What was the total weight of the three fish reported?

Check your answers
on page 112.

LESSON 9   Subtracting Decimals

Valerie sold 1.8 million dollars worth of homes and properties last year. This year, she sold 2.3 million dollars worth of real estate. Valerie wants to know how much more her sales are this year? Valerie subtracts to find the answer.

	1 13
This year's sales	2.3
Last year's sales	− 1.8
	.5

The illustration above shows how Valerie subtracted to find how much more money she made in sales. This procedure is the same as subtracting whole numbers, but the decimal points must be in a straight column.

EXAMPLE 1

32.8 − 15.5 = ?

Valerie's client wants to put up a wall to separate the living room and dining room. The room is 32.8 feet long. They want to make the dining room 15.5 feet long. How long will the living room be?

Step 1   Set up the problem vertically. Write a decimal point for each number in a column, one point directly under the other. Write a decimal point for the answer directly under the other decimal points. Write a subtraction sign.

$$\begin{array}{r} . \\ -\ . \\ \hline . \end{array}$$

Step 2   Write the numbers with decimal points. Keep the tenths to the right of the decimal point and the whole numbers to the left.

$$\begin{array}{r} 32.8 \\ -15.5 \\ \hline . \end{array}$$

Step 3   Work the problem. Subtract the tenths: 8 − 5 = 3. Regroup 1 ten to make 10 ones. Cross out the 3 in the tens column and write a 2 above it. Cross out the 2 in the ones column. Regroup the ones: 10 + 2 = 12. Write a 12 above the ones column. Subtract the ones: 12 − 5 = 7. Subtract the tens: 2 − 1 = 1.

$$\begin{array}{r} {}^{2\ 12}\cancel{3}\cancel{2}.8 \\ -15.5 \\ \hline 17.3 \end{array}$$

EXERCISE 9A

Write the numbers in columns. Then subtract.

1. 9.3 − 6.4 = ?

2. 38.1 − 22.5 = ?

3. 70.6 − 49.7 = ?

4. 531.9 − 286.4 = ?

APPLICATION

Check your answers on page 113.

5. The interest rate for a conventional home loan is 9.8 percent for a fixed, thirty-year loan. Valerie expects that the rates will drop 1.2 percent by the end of the year. What will the loan rate be if the rates drop?

Subtracting Hundredths

To subtract numbers that have hundredths, follow the same procedure of subtracting decimals, but start by subtracting the hundredths first.

EXAMPLE 2

$73.04 - 38.51 = ?$

Step 1 Set up the problem vertically. Write the decimal points for the numbers and the answer in a straight line. Write the subtraction sign.

$$\begin{array}{r} . \\ -. \\ \hline . \end{array}$$

Step 2 Write the numbers with the decimal points.

$$\begin{array}{r} 73.04 \\ -38.51 \\ \hline . \end{array}$$

Step 3 Subtract the hundredths column. Subtract the tenths column. Subtract the ones column. Subtract the tens column. Regroup when you need to.

$$\begin{array}{r} 7\overset{6}{\cancel{3}}\overset{12}{\cancel{}}.0\overset{10}{\cancel{4}} \\ -38.51 \\ \hline 34.53 \end{array}$$

EXERCISE 9B

Write the numbers in columns. Then subtract.

6. $2.62 - 1.95 = ?$

7. $31.46 - 20.79 = ?$

8. $91.84 - 75.03 = ?$

9. $639.41 - 507.16 = ?$

APPLICATION

10. Valerie has a client who owns 364.52 acres of land. They want to sell all of it except 108.73 acres. How many acres will Valerie list for sale?

Check your answers on page 113.

MATH TIP To subtract decimals with numbers in the thousandths or smaller, follow the same procedure. Begin subtracting the column on the right. Remember to keep the decimal points in a straight column when rewriting the problem.

USE WHAT YOU HAVE LEARNED

Write the numbers in columns. Then subtract.

1. 27.3 − 18.1 = ?

2. 49.62 − 25.95 = ?

3. 59.004 − 16.293 = ?

APPLICATIONS

4. Alberto is a weight trainer at the gym. One of the dumbbells has 31.4 pounds of weight on it. His client wants to warm up by curling only 18.2 pounds of weight. How much weight will Alberto remove from the dumbbells?

5. Imelda spends $36.29 at the office supply store. Including tax, $11.54 of the bill is for merchandise she buys for the office. The rest is for merchandise she buys for home use. How much money did Imelda spend for home use?

6. The highway department has paved 28.58 miles of a road that will be 47.38 miles long when it is done. How much road does the highway department have left to pave?

7. Dan oversees the recycling program for his office. Between the paper products and the aluminum cans, he had collected a total of 321.93 pounds. The weight of the cans was 167.04 pounds. How much of the weight was paper products?

8. Jack is hanging a banner in front of a store. The banner is 10.7 feet wide. The ropes are 12.5 feet long. The total height of the building is 34.3 feet high. How far off the ground will the bottom of the banner be?

9. Martin needs to cut a board that is 4.75 feet long. He also needs one that is 2.55 feet long. Will a board that is 7.33 feet be long enough to cut both pieces? If not, how much too short is the board? If so, how much more will he have to cut off?

Check your answers on page 113.

LESSON 10 Subtracting Decimals with Different Place Values

Sam drives a truck for a concrete company. He is to deliver 4.8 cubic yards of concrete for a sidewalk. His truck holds 9 cubic yards of concrete. Sam wants to know how much concrete will be left in the truck for the next job. Sam subtracts to find how much concrete will be left in his truck.

$$
\begin{array}{r}
{\scriptstyle 8\ 10} \\
9.\cancel{0} \\
-\ 4.8 \\
\hline
4.2
\end{array}
$$

The problem above shows how Sam subtracted to find the amount of concrete left in his truck. Sam wrote a decimal point and a zero to help him subtract the numbers. Adding zeros to the right of the decimal point does not change the value of the number ($3 = $3.00), and it helps keep the columns aligned. This procedure will be the same whenever you subtract decimals with different place values.

EXAMPLE 1

4.2 − 3 = ?

Sam knows he has 4.2 cubic yards of concrete in his truck after pouring the sidewalk. He is to go to another house and pour a pad for a garden shed. He will need 3 cubic yards. How much concrete will be left in his truck then?

$$
\begin{array}{cccc}
. & 4.2 & 4.2 & 4.2 \\
-. & -3. & -3.0 & -3.0 \\
\hline
. & . & . & 1.2 \\
\text{Step 1} & \text{Step 2} & \text{Step 3} & \text{Step 4}
\end{array}
$$

Step 1   Set up the problem vertically. Write a decimal point for each number and line them up in a column. Include a decimal point for the whole number 3. Because the number being subtracted has decimal value, it will be necessary to add zeros to the right of the decimal in the whole number 3. Write another decimal point directly under the other points in the answer. Write the subtraction sign.

Step 2   Write in the numbers with the decimal point. Keep the tenths to the right of the decimal point and the whole numbers to the left of the deciaml point.

Step 3   Write a 0 in the tenths column beside the 3. The 0 shows there are no tenths and makes the columns even.

Step 4   Subtract the tenths column: 2 − 0 = 2. Write the 2 in the tenths column. Subtract the ones column: 4 − 3 = 1. Write the 1 in the ones column.

EXERCISE 10A

Write the numbers in columns. Then subtract.

1. $7 - 2.3 = ?$

2. $13.5 - 11 = ?$

3. $86 - 47.9 = ?$

4. $74.3 - .9 = ?$

APPLICATION

Check your answers on page 113.

5. Sam has directions telling him how to get to a house that ordered concrete. He is to drive 18 miles from the plant before turning right into the subdivision. He has already driven 15.4 miles. How much further does Sam need to go before he turns?

Subtracting Hundredths

When subtracting numbers with differing decimal place values, write a 0 in each decimal column to help keep the columns aligned. Then subtract, starting with the hundredths column.

EXAMPLE 2

$89 - 31.53 = ?$

Step 1 Set up the problem vertically. Write a decimal point for each number. Make sure to line the points up. Write a decimal for the answer directly under them. Write the subtraction sign.

$$\begin{array}{r} . \\ -\ . \\ \hline . \end{array}$$

Step 2 Write in the numbers with the decimal points.

$$\begin{array}{r} 89. \\ -31.53 \\ \hline . \end{array}$$

Step 3 Write two zeroes for place holders beside the first number, one for the tenths column and one for the hundredths column.

$$\begin{array}{r} 89.00 \\ -31.53 \\ \hline . \end{array}$$

Step 4 Subtract the hundredths column. Subtract the tenths column. Subtract the ones column. Subtract the tens column. Regroup when you need to.

$$\begin{array}{r} \overset{8}{\cancel{8}}\overset{9}{\cancel{9}}\overset{10}{\cancel{0}} \\ 89.00 \\ -31.53 \\ \hline 57.47 \end{array}$$

EXERCISE 10B

Write the numbers in columns. Then subtract.

6. 8 − .14 = ?

7. 54.8 − 15.03 = ?

8. 67 − 21.44 = ?

9. 50.47 − 3.9 = ?

APPLICATION

Check your answers
on page 114.

10. Beverly drives a taxi. She drives three people from the airport to a hotel. The meter shows that the passengers owe her $11.78. One of the people gives her a $20 bill. How much change will Beverly give back?

MATH TIP

To help keep the decimal columns aligned, use zeros so that the numbers have the same place value. Then subtract.

USE WHAT YOU HAVE LEARNED

Write the numbers in columns. Then subtract.

1. 12 − 4.9 = ?

2. 56.2 − 30 = ?

3. 80.31 − 77.4 = ?

4. 61 − 9.58 = ?

5. 32.6 − 15.08 = ?

6. 43 − 20.07 = ?

7. 6 − 2.148 = ?

8. 38.17 − .543 = ?

APPLICATIONS

9. Lionel installs mirrors and glass for showers. He measures a wall that is 60.45 inches wide for a mirror. The customer wants the mirror to cover as much of the wall as possible. There is an electrical outlet on one end of the wall. Lionel wants to allow 9.8 inches for the outlet. How long will Lionel make the mirror?

10. Max is a butcher in a small meat market. A customer selects a 23.38 pound sirloin tip. She asks Max to cut it into a 7.5 pound roast and steaks totaling 9 pounds. She wants the remainder ground into hamburger. When Max repackaged the meat, what weight did he write on the hamburger?

11. Claire works in a clothes store. A customer buys $145.92 worth of merchandise. The customer wants to pay 50 dollars of it in cash and write a check for the remainder. How much should the customer write the check for?

12. Pete needs to order wood to make a set of office cabinets. The plans show that the doors on the bottom are 23.25 inches long by 26.5 inches wide. There is a 2-inch trim around the inset panel of the doors. Pete needs to know how wide to make the inset panel to order the right width of wood. What is the width of the panel?

13. Juan is framing a house with 10 foot ceilings. One room will have a window that is 6 feet tall. The drawing shows the window placed 1.8 feet from the floor. When Juan frames the window, what is the total length from the ceiling to the top of the window?

14. Tran works in a picture framing shop. She measures a print and finds that the length is 24.8 inches and the width is 19.06 inches. The framing material is eight feet, or 96 inches, long. Can Tran make the frame by using one length of framing material? If not, how many inches short is the wood? If so, how many inches will Tran have left over?

Check your answers
on page 115.

CHAPTER 2 Summary

When you add or subtract decimals, it is important to keep the decimal points and columns aligned. If you are working with decimals with different place values, then it is helpful to use zeros to make the place values the same.

EXERCISE A

Write the following addition problems in columns and then add.

1. .3 + .4 =

2. .26 + .33 =

3. . 27 + .67 =

4. .678 + .224 =

5. .88 + .77 =

6. .456 + .789 =

7. 2.47 + 22.98 =

8. 4.893 + 56.87 =

9. 2.789 + 456.7 =

10. .36 + 27 + 2.365 =

11. $738.1 + .478 + 4 =$ **12.** $765.098 + .3 + 354 =$

Check your answers
on page 115.

EXERCISE B

Write the following subtraction problems in columns and then subtract.

13. $.36 - .11 =$ **14.** $.439 - .328 =$

15. $.468 - .056 =$ **16.** $.723 - .488 =$

17. $7.873 - .972 =$ **18.** $23.453 - 19.476 =$

19. $53.87 - 5.879 =$ **20.** $27.98 - .997 =$

Check your answers
on page 116.

MATH AT WORK

1. **Delivery Driver** Allen has collected gas receipts for 8.29, 9.0, and 10.50 gallons this week. What is his total amount of gasoline bought?

2. **Secretary** Maryanne bought office supplies including an invoice book at $2.99, a two-inch stamp at $2.29, and two stamp pads at $2.69. How much did she spend?

3. **Machine Operator** Manuel operates a trencher. Manuel's crew is scheduled to lay 126 miles of drainage pipe along highways. They have completed 53.57 miles. How much is left to complete?

4. **Retail Clerk** Claire is writing up a sale in the computer store. The customer has purchased a computer on sale for $1,599.99 and has $225.00 in cash. How much should she charge him on his credit card?

5. **Carpenter** Ernie is laying baseboard molding in a room 10.6' x 12.6'. How many feet of baseboard molding will he need to complete the job?

6. **Delivery Driver** Bob must deliver 3 washing machines. His projected round trip drive time is one hour and twenty minutes for the first delivery, 30 minutes for the second delivery, and two hours for the third delivery. He must also budget 30 minutes for set-up and installation with each delivery. How many hours will Bob work today?

MATH AT WORK

7. Delivery Driver Zach drives a recycling delivery truck. The truck weighs 20,555 lb. empty and 21,432.8 lb. when he drives it on the scale at the end of the day. The aluminum cans he off loads weigh 339.9 lb. How much does the remaining newspaper weigh?

8. Butcher Max the butcher is preparing an order for Mrs. Jones. She has ordered 10.5 lb. brisket, twelve 8 ounce steaks, and 4.25 lb. of ground beef. How much does her total order weigh?

9. Retail Clerk Jennie works in a candy store. Three types of candy are on sale for $1.55 per pound. Mrs. Smith asks for two and one quarter pounds of gummy bears, one and one half pounds of squirmy worms, and one and sixty-five hundredths of a pound of gum drops. How many pounds of candy did she order?

10. Laboratory Technician Edward times three chemical reactions in the lab. The first reaction takes 7.94 seconds; the second takes 8.455 seconds; and the third takes 8.01 seconds. What is the total time of these three chemical reactions, rounded to the nearest hundredth?

11. Events Coordinator Beth is the events coordinator for The Children's Fund. She is arranging a fund-raising picnic. She intends to hang a banner 12.75 feet wide between two telephone poles that are 32.6 feet apart. She wants to tie streamers to the rope that supports the banner. How much rope will be left uncovered by the banner?

12. Retail Clerk A customer buys $153.69 worth of merchandise at the hardware store and presents two one hundred dollar bills to pay for it. How much change should Iris give him?

13. Carpenter   Pete is building a patio deck. He needs twenty 12 ft. planks. He will lay the planks side by side to create a deck that is 10.5 feet long. How much will he have to cut off (a) each plank and (b) in total?

14. Contractor   Quality of Life Home Builders are adding a sunroom to a house. They need four panes of window glass 6.75 ft by 4.75 ft. How much wood molding will they need to frame these windows?

15. File Clerk   Mary has responsibility for petty cash in her office. This month she has a starting balance of $25.14 and pays amounts of $1.49, $2.55 and $9.89. How much does she have left at the end of the month?

16. Retail Clerk   Sam, who works in the fresh fish department of a grocery store, is asked to weigh a customer's order. It included one whole salmon weighing ten pounds and forty-four hundredths of a pound; three catfish totaling six pounds and fifty-four hundredths of a pound and 3.89 lb. of shrimp. What is the total weight?

17. Accountant   Betty Lou has the responsibility of balancing the company checkbook. Her starting balance is $1,023.56. During this month two deposits of $50.00 and $450.00 were made. Checks were written for $68.79, $15.99, and $9.00. What is the balance at the end of the month?

18. Salesperson   Sam sells pipe fittings and has an expense account to take clients out to lunch. He started the month with $100 in this account. He took three clients out to lunch, costing him $21.89, $15.77, and $25.50. How much money does he have left?

19. Retail Clerk   Nancy works in a jewelry store that sells gold chains by weight. A customer selects three chains weighing .557 gm, .749 gm, and 1.250 gm. What is the total weight in grams?

20. Payroll Clerk   Maria is adding time cards in the payroll department. Jesus's time cards shows 8.25, 9., 8.5, 9.0 and 8.25 for the week. What are his total hours for the week?

21. Secretary   Al keeps track of cash donations to the office coffee pot. His daily collections for last week were $.43, $2.35, $1.85, $1.95. $2.10. If a can of coffee costs $3.95, sugar costs $.89, and cream costs $1.23, then are the donations enough to cover the coffee-pot expenses?

22. Maintenance Supervisor   Some workers on Matt's shift are careless with tools. He had to replace one hammer at $16.89, one hack saw and blades for $12.95, and two screwdrivers for $3.99. How much did the carelessness of the workers cost his company?

23. Salesperson   Tom's client visits take one hour and forty-two hundredths, 1 hour and fifty-five hundredths, two hours and two hours and twenty-five hundredths. What is the total amount of time spent on client visits?

24. Shipping Clerk   Yolanda, in the shipping department, weighed the following packages: 15.29 lb., 2.333 lb. 5.50 lb. How much did these three packages weigh?

Check your answers on page 116.

Multiplication with Decimals

LESSON 11 Multiplying Decimals

Bill was just hired by the city. On his way home to tell his wife, he figures out how much he will earn each week. He will work 40 hours per week and earn $8.33 an hour. Bill multiplies $8.33 × 40 so he can tell his wife how much he will be making.

Multiplying Decimals

Multiplying decimals is similar to multiplying whole numbers. Place the decimal point in your answer after you multiply.

EXAMPLE 1

Multiply $8.33 × 49

$$
\begin{array}{r} \$8.33 \\ \times 40 \\ \hline \end{array}
\qquad
\begin{array}{r} \$8.33 \\ \times 40 \\ \hline 000 \\ +33320 \\ \hline 33320 \end{array}
\qquad
\begin{array}{r} \$8.33 \\ \times 40 \\ \hline 000 \\ +33320 \\ \hline 333.20 \end{array}
\qquad \$333.20
$$

Step 1   Step 2   Step 3   (2 places)

Step 1 Bill lines up the numbers he needs to multiply like other multiplication problems he has worked and multiplies.

Step 2 He adds the partial products.

Step 3 Bill inserts the decimal point in the answer (333.20) two places from the right, since the number 8.33 has two number places to the right of the decimal point. Move the decimal point in the product the same number of places as the total number of decimal places contained in the numbers being multiplied.

MATH TIP

When multiplying numbers with decimals, place the decimal points **after** you finish multiplying. Count the total number of places to the right of the decimal point in **both** of the numbers being multiplied. Place the decimal point that number of spaces from the right in the answer.

EXERCISE 11

Convert the following into vertical multiplication problems. Multiply. Remember to place the decimal point in your answer.

1. $10.00 × 4 =

2. 7.889 × 8 =

3. 43.093 × 55 =

4. 93.035 × 28 =

APPLICATION

Check your answers on page 120.

5. Assuming that each month has a minimum of 4 weeks, what is the least Bill will earn in any one month?

MATH TIP

Remember to count the total number of places in **both** numbers being multiplied. Look at the example at right. The number being multiplied has two decimal places, and the multiplier has one decimal place. Therefore, the product contains three decimal places.

```
    2.45
 ×  1.3
    735
+2450
  3.185
```

USE WHAT YOU HAVE LEARNED

1. Multiply
6.5 × 7 =

2. Multiply
9.09 × 12 =

3. Multiply
21.93 × 34 =

4. Multiply
439.088 × 58 =

5. Multiply
45.7904 × 72 =

6. Multiply
399.032 × 2.46=

7. Multiply
87.4235 × 4.9 =

8. Multiply
666.094 × .3902=

APPLICATIONS

9. Remembering that Bill makes $333.20 per week, how much money does he make in a year? (Hint: There are 52 weeks in a year.)

10. Pierre's car payment is $180.69 each month for 36 months. How much will he pay altogether?

11. A recycling center pays $0.124 per pound for plastic. How much will be paid for 202.3 pounds?

12. It costs $0.28 per mile to rent a van. What is the cost if you drive it 121.7 miles?

13. A nurse earns $11.25 per hour. What is her weekly pay for a 40-hour week?

14. Last week, the same nurse worked 15 hours of overtime at a rate of $15.90. How much overtime pay did she earn?

15. What was the total paycheck for the week of the nurse described in the previous two questions?

Check your answers
on page 120.

LESSON 12 Multiplication by 10, 100, 1,000

Guillermo runs his own pizza business. He has gone to the wholesale store to pick up disposable supplies such as paper towels, toilet paper, and note pads. A case of paper towels costs $14.18. Guillermo needs to know the cost of 10 cases.

Multiplying Decimals by 10, 100, 1,000

Multiplying decimals by 10, 100, and 1,000 is simplified because decimals are based on powers of ten. The decimal point moves one place to the right for every zero in the multiplier. Below, you see the same mixed decimal (14.18) multiplied by 10, 100, and 1,000.

$$
\begin{array}{r}
14.18 \\
\times 10 \\
\hline
0 \\
14180 \\
\hline
141.80
\end{array}
\qquad
\begin{array}{r}
14.18 \\
\times 100 \\
\hline
0 \\
00 \\
141800 \\
\hline
1{,}418.00
\end{array}
\qquad
\begin{array}{r}
14.18 \\
\times 1000 \\
\hline
0 \\
00 \\
000 \\
1418000 \\
\hline
14{,}180.00
\end{array}
$$

14.18 becomes 141.8   14.18 becomes 1,418   14.18 becomes 14,180

$$
\begin{array}{c}
141.8 \\
\times 10
\end{array}
\qquad
\begin{array}{c}
14.18. \\
\times 100
\end{array}
\qquad
\begin{array}{c}
14.180. \\
\times 1{,}000
\end{array}
$$

EXAMPLE 1

Multiply 14.18 × 1,000

Step 1 Count the number of zeros in the multiplier. 1,000 has 3 zeros.

14.18 × 1,000 =

Step 2 Locate the decimal point in the number being multiplied. Move the decimal point 1 place to the right for each zero in the multiplier.

14.18 × 1,000 = 14.18_.

Step 3 In this case, since a place has been created, fill the place with a zero.

14.18 × 1,000 = 14,180.

EXERCISE 12

Use mental math to multiply the following.

1. $5.25 × 10 =

2. $14.55 × 100 =

3. $.33 \times 1000 =$ **4.** $7.089 \times 10 =$

APPLICATION

Check your answers
on page 121.

5. Maria's local copy center charges $ .035 per page for copies. How much would she be charged for 1000 copies? Use mental math.

You can use mental math to multiply by 10, 100, or 1,000. Move the decimal point 1 place to the right for every zero in the multiplier.

USE WHAT YOU HAVE LEARNED

Use mental math to compute the following.

1. Multiply
   $3.9 \times 10 =$

2. Multiply
   $6.7 \times 10 =$

3. Multiply
   $5.9 \times 100 =$

4. Multiply
   $9.5 \times 100 =$

5. Multiply
   $69.3 \times 10 =$

6. Multiply
   $5.8 \times 100 =$

7. Multiply
   $4.19 \times 100 =$

8. Multiply
   $7.27 \times 1000 =$

9. Multiply
   $70.35 \times 100 =$

10. Multiply
   $67.02 \times 100 =$

11. Multiply
   $30.09 \times 1000 =$

12. Multiply
   $6694.1 \times 1000 =$

13. Multiply
   $\$6.75 \times 100 =$

14. Multiply
   $3.45 \times 10 =$

15. Multiply
   $90.60 \times 1000 =$

16. Multiply
   $.87 \times 100 =$

17. Multiply
   $3.89 \times 1000 =$

18. Multiply
   $55.89 \times 10 =$

19. Multiply
   $\$4.85 \times 1000 =$

20. Multiply
   $\$10.75 \times 10 =$

APPLICATIONS

21. Edward has to gas up the delivery vans before they head out for their morning runs. He pumps ten gallons into each of the eight vans.

    How many gallons does he pump each day?

    In a five-day week, how many gallons does he pump?

    His supervisor wants two-week records kept. How many gallons does Edward pump in ten days?

    His supervisor pays $1.129 per gallon. How much money does it cost him to gas up the fleet every two weeks?

22. Sandoz packages pencils in groups of 100 at her factory job. At a cost of $.04 per pencil, how much does one package of pencils cost?

23. The more pencils a customer buys, the lower the cost. If a customer wants 1,000 pencils, Sandoz's company sells them for $.03 each. How much will be charged?

24. If copies cost $.043 each, how much do 10 copies cost? How much do 100 copies cost? How much do 1,000 copies cost? Use mental math.

25. The sales tax on office supplies is $ .074 for each dollar. How much money can Mark save on $100 of office supplies if he buys his supplies from a vendor with no sales tax?

Check your answers
on page 121.

LESSON 13 Multiplication by .1, .01, .001

Nadia works for a large company that makes men's shirts. She is paid an hourly wage of $7.25. She is expected to work at least eight hours per day, five days a week. The company pays $10.88 per hour for overtime. However, the time clock is very specific and computes overtime in tenths of an hour. On Monday, Nadia stayed 6 minutes beyond quitting time to finish a special order. Nadia wants to know how much she earned for her one tenth of an hour of overtime.

Multiplying by .1, .01, .001

When multiplying by .1 $\left(\frac{1}{10}\right)$, .01 $\left(\frac{1}{100}\right)$, and .001 $\left(\frac{1}{1000}\right)$, the decimal point moves one place to the left for each decimal place in the multiplier. Below, you see the same mixed decimal (10.88) multiplied by .1, .01, and .001.

EXAMPLE 1

Multiply 10.88 × .001

$$
\begin{array}{ccc}
10.88 & 10.88 & 10.88 \\
\underline{\times .1 \text{ one place}} & \underline{\times .01 \text{ two places}} & \underline{\times .001 \text{ three places}} \\
1.088 & .1088 & .01088
\end{array}
$$

10.88 becomes 1.088   10.88 becomes .1088   10.88 becomes .01088

Step 1 Count the number of decimal places in the multiplier. .001 has three decimal places.

$10.88 \times .001 =$

Step 2 Locate the decimal point in the number being multiplied. Move the decimal point one place to the left for each decimal place in the multiplier.

$10.88 \times .001 = .\_10.88$

Step 3 In this case, since a place has been created, fill the place with a zero.

$10.88 \times .001 = .01088$

EXERCISE 13

Use mental math to multiply the following.

1. $7.25 × .1 =$ **2.** $10.88 × .01 =$ **3.** 3.44 × .001 =

APPLICATION

Check your answers
on page 122.

4. One hundred empty soda cans weigh 4.5 pounds. How much does one can weigh?

MATH TIP

Use mental math to multiply by .1, .01, or .001. Move the decimal point one place to the left for every decimal place in the multiplier. Multiplying by .1, .01, and .001 is the same as dividing by 10, 100, or 1000.

USE WHAT YOU HAVE LEARNED

Use mental math to multiply the following.

1. $2.3 \times .01 =$

2. $.46 \times 0.01 =$

3. $260 \times .001 =$

4. $.003 \times .01 =$

APPLICATIONS

5. The cost of operating an electric motor for one hour is $0.035. How much does it cost to operate it for .1 hour?

6. A certain fertilizer must be used at the rate 3.55 gallons per acre. How much is needed for one tenth of an acre?

7. Darian was charged $53.00 for 1000 copies at the copy center. How much did each copy cost?

8. Gayle found .03 grams of pollen in the collector of the air filtration system in her building. This was 100 times the acceptable limits prescribed by the safety office. How many grams of pollen were considered acceptable by the safety office?

9. Brian is looking for the ramp onto the freeway. He is making his last delivery of the day. He sees a sign saying his exit is .5 miles ahead. At 60 miles per hour, how long does he have before he misses his exit?

10. Dora's company offers a profit-sharing dividend of $28,000 to be divided equally among the thousand participants in the profit-sharing plan. How much can Dora expect to receive?

Check your answers
on page 122.

LESSON 14 Working with the Metric System

Words to KNOW

A *prefix* is a word or group of letters attached to the beginning of another word. The metric system uses a standard set of prefixes attached to its basic units of measurement to show number.

Martin is a mechanic. He imports a special type of motor oil for his customers who drive expensive German cars. He has been buying oil by the case, twelve 1-liter bottles at a time. Because he is using more oil than he used to, however, he is thinking of buying it in bulk in a 2-hectoliter barrel. He knows that it typically takes 5 liters of oil to do an oil change. He needs to find out how many oil changes he can get out of a barrel to know if it is worthwhile keeping this much oil on hand.

Working with Metric Measurements

Martin realizes that if he can determine how many liters there are in 2 hectoliters, he will be able to get a sense of how much oil 2 hectoliters is.

Prefix	kilo	hecto	deca (or deka)	unit	deci	centi	milli
multiplier	×1000	×100	×10	meter (m)	×.1	×.01	×.001
symbol	k	h	da	liter (l)	d	c	m
				gram (g)			

EXAMPLE 1

2 hectoliters = how many liters?

Step 1 Consult the chart above. Find the **prefix** "hecto."

Step 2 Recognize that "hecto" means 100 × whatever the basic unit of measurement is. Hecto means you should move the decimal point two places to the right (1.0 liters becomes 100 liters, or 1 hectoliter).

Step 3 Since there are 2 hectoliters in a barrel, multiply 100 × 2. Two hectoliters is 200 liters.

If you are measuring the length of something, then 1 hectometer is 100 meters. If you are measuring the weight of something, then 1 hectogram is 100 grams. In this case, you are measuring the volume of something. The metric unit of measurement for volume is the liter. A hectoliter is 100 liters.

EXERCISE 14

Supply the correct unit of measurement.

1. The metric unit that measures weight is the _____ .

2. The metric unit that measures length is the _____ .

3. The metric unit that measures volume is the _____ .

Supply the correct prefix.

4. _____ means 100 ×

5. _____ means .01 ×

6. _____ means 10 ×

7. _____ means .1 ×

8. _____ means 1000 ×

9. _____ means .001 ×

Convert the following.

10. 4 kilometers = _____meters

11. 5 centimeters = _____ meters

12. 5 decaliters = _____ liters

13. 2 deciliters = _____ liters

14. 22 hectograms = _____ grams

15. 3 centigrams = _____ grams

APPLICATION

16. Bob orders a hectoliter of propane for his kiln. The kiln uses an average of a deciliter per hour. How many hours' worth of running time can Bob count on before he runs out of fuel?

Check your answers on page 122.

To successfully work in the decimal system, you must learn the prefixes. Once you do, computation of different lengths, weights, and volumes can be accomplished by moving decimal points.

USE WHAT YOU HAVE LEARNED

Convert the following.

1. 2 kiloliters = _____ deciliters

2. 3 centimeters = _____ decimeters

3. 4 hectometers = _____ millimeters

4. 2 decagrams = _____ decigrams

5. 11 hectoliters = _____ milliliters

6. 12 milligrams = _____ decagrams

APPLICATIONS

7. Marsha is told by a doctor to provide a patient intravenous fluids at the rate of 20 centiliters per hour for the next 5 hours. How many liters of solution will she need?

8. Bill must place a center reflector every 10 meters along a stretch of road. How many reflectors will he place per kilometer?

9. Jordan notes that there are 5 grams of fat in every serving of pasta. How many kilograms will there be in 100 servings?

10. Brittany has a full tub of ink paste weighing a kilogram, a partial tub containing 30 grams of ink paste, and 5 centigrams of ink paste in her printer's reservoir. How much ink paste does she have in all?

11. Clyde buys toner by the kilogram. How much would be left in a 1-kilogram bottle if Clyde put 45 centigrams of toner in his copier?

12. Mark buys .75 liter of bottled insecticide concentrate. When mixed with water, 75 milliliters makes 1 full liter of chemical for spraying. How many liters of spray can Mark get from the bottle of concentrate?

13. Shaunté is a hairstylist. Her favorite conditioner comes in 875-milliliter bottles. How many liters is this?

Check your answers on page 123.

LESSON 15 Scientific Notation

Words to KNOW

An *exponent* is a small number written above and to the right of a number. It signifies the number of times the lower number, the *base*, is being multiplied by itself.

Dulcey works in a products-testing lab. Today she is testing engine lubricants. The test specifications state that each lubricant is to be left inside a running engine for 5 hours or a minimum of 9.2×10^5 revolutions of the engine.

Exponents

The number, 9.2×10^5, is an example of a way of writing very large numbers called *scientific notation*. But before you can understand scientific notation, you must learn about **exponents**.

Exponents are small numbers written above and to the right of another number. The number they are written next to is called the **base**. In Dulcey's case, 10 is the base and ^{5} is the exponent.

EXAMPLE 1

Convert 10^5 to a whole number.

$$10^5 = 10 \times 10 \times 10 \times 10 \times 10$$

$$10 \times 10 = 100$$
$$100 \times 10 = 1,000$$
$$1,000 \times 10 = 10,000$$
$$10,000 \times 10 = 100,000$$

$$10^5 = 100,000$$

Step 1   Step 2   Step 3

Step 1   Write out the exponentiated number as a multiplication problem. 10^5 means five tens multiplied together.

Step 2   Do the multiplication. Follow through the example, and count the tens. Ten has been multiplied 5 times.

Step 3   Rewrite the expression.

Exponents can be used with any number.

$$3^3 = 3 \times 3 \times 3 = 9 \times 3 = 27,$$
$$\text{or}$$
$$7^4 = 7 \times 7 \times 7 \times 7 = 49 \times 7 \times 7 = 343 \times 7 = 2,401$$

EXERCISE 15A

Convert the following exponentiated numbers into whole numbers.

1. $2^6 =$ **2.** $4^3 =$ **3.** $6^3 =$ **4.** $3^5 =$

Check your answers on page 123.

APPLICATION

5. Marvin buys 1 cubic yard of mulch. A cubic yard is 1^3 yards. A yard is equal to 3 feet. How many cubic feet are there in a cubic yard?

Scientific Notation

Scientific notation is a way to write very large numbers in a smaller space. Scientific notation uses exponents to take advantage of the unique multiplication properties of 10.

Remember Dulcey's specification and its use of 9.2×10^5. Look back at Step 2 of Example 1. Every time you multiply by 10, you move the decimal place 1 place to the right. With whole numbers, you add a zero.

Now count the number of zeros behind the 1 in 100,000. There are 5, just like the exponent in 10^5. The exponent tells you how many decimal places you need to move to the right if the base is 10.

EXAMPLE 2

Convert 9.2×10^5 into a whole number.

Step 1	Move the decimal point in 9.2 five (exponent = 5) places to the right.	9.2×10^5 $9.2\_\_\_\_\_$
Step 2	Since you've created places, fill in the places with zeros.	$920,000.$ $10^5 = 10 \times 10 \times 10 \times 10 \times 10$ $= 100,000$
Step 3	Confirm this result by multiplying out the exponentiated number.	$\times\ 9.2$ $920,000$

EXERCISE 15B

Convert the following numbers expressed in scientific notation into whole numbers.

6. 4.2×10^5 **7.** 4.34×10^7

8. $.15 \times 10^6$ **9.** 78.3×10^5

APPLICATION

Check your answers on page 124.

10. Tom wants to buy a gas station. The prospectus says the intersection it is located on has an annual traffic flow of 3.744×10^6 vehicles. How many vehicles is this?

MATH TIP

When an exponent indicates a large number of multiplications, it is often helpful to group your factors. Take 2^8 for example.

$$2^8 = 2 \times 2 \times 2 \times 2 \times 2 \times 2 \times 2 \times 2 =$$

$$2^8 = (2 \times 2) \times (2 \times 2) \times (2 \times 2) \times (2 \times 2) = \text{Group the 2s}$$

$(4 \times 4) \qquad \times \qquad (4 \times 4) \qquad$ = Group the twos into 4 fours

$16 \qquad \times \qquad 16 \qquad$ and then finally into 2 sixteens.

$= 256$

Also, 2^8 means 8 twos multiplied together, not 8×2. The most common error involving exponents comes about when you multiply the base by the exponent. In this example you multiply $2 \times 2 \times 2 \times 2 \times 2 \times 2 \times 2 \times 2$, not 2×8.

USE WHAT YOU HAVE LEARNED

Convert the following into whole numbers.

1. 5^2

2. 4^3

3. 9^4

4. 6^5

5. 4.3×10^5

6. 6×10^6

7. 7.004×10^7

8. 3.12×10^8

APPLICATIONS

9. Neut sees that the shipping department used 4.3×10^4 feet of strapping tape last year. In whole numbers, how many feet of tape was this?

10. Gladys was asked to build cubical photographic risers. Each box was described as 2^3 feet. What was the length of each side of each riser?

11. The scale on Paula's map was given as 1 to 2.234×10^6. In whole numbers, the scale of the map was 1 to what?

12. Jerome needed to know how many cubic inches there were in a cubic yard. He knew there were 36 inches in a yard. But what is 36^3?

13. Bonita is thinking of opening a part-time radio repair business to earn a little money. She sees an estimate that there are around 3.9×10^6 radios owned by people in her city of 650,000. How many radios is this?

14. While looking through a box of old electronics parts, Bonita finds a resistor labeled 2.2×10^5 ohms. How many ohms is this?

Check your answers
on page 124.

CHAPTER 3 Summary

Multiplying decimals

When multiplying numbers with decimals, place the decimal points after you finish multiplying. Count the total number of places to the right of the decimal point in both of the numbers being multiplied. Place the decimal point that number of spaces from the right in the answer.

EXERCISE A

Multiply.

1. $20.00 × 3 =

2. 6.778 × 7 =

3. 52.104 × 66 =

4. 82.024 × 17 =

5. 8.5 × 8 =

6. 6.06 × 14 =

7. 13.43 × 41 =

8. 4.098 × 52 =

9. 19.45 × .23 =

Check your answers on page 124.

10. 421.89 × 2.61 =

11. 99.422 × .49 =

12. 611.09 × 3.4 =

Multiplication by 10, 100, and 1,000

To multiply by 10, 100, or 1,000, move the decimal point 1 place to the right for every zero in the multiplier. Add zeros to the right to fill the places created.

EXERCISE B

Multiply.

13. 69.3 × 10 =

14. 5.8 × 100 =

Check your answers on page 125.

15. 4.19 × 100 =

16. 7.27 × 1,000 =

Multiplication by .1, .01, and .001

To multiply by .1, .01, or .001, move the decimal point 1 place to the left for every decimal place in the multiplier. Add zeros to the left to fill the places created.

EXERCISE C

Multiply.

17. 58.4 × .1 =

18. 6.9 × .01 =

Check your answers on page 125.

19. 2.21 × .01 =

20. 8.37 × .001 =

Working in the Metric System

To successfully work in the decimal system you must learn to recognize the metric prefixes. These prefixes are illustrated in the chart below. Each column is 10 × more than the column on its right. Computation of different lengths, weights, and volumes can be accomplished by simply moving decimal points.

Prefix	kilo	hecto	deca (or deka)	unit	deci	centi	milli
multiplier	×1000	×100	×10	meter (m)	×.1	×.01	×.001
symbol	k	h	da	liter (l)	d	c	m
				gram (g)			

EXERCISE D

Convert the following.

21. 2 kilometers = _____ meters

22. 4 centigrams = _____ decigrams

23. 6 hectoliters = _____ centiliters

Check your answers on page 125.

24. 3 decameters = _____ decimeters

Scientific Notation

Scientific notation is a way to write very large numbers in a smaller space. Scientific notation uses exponents to take advantage of the unique multiplication properties of 10.

EXERCISE E

Convert the following into conventional whole numbers.

25. 2.4×10^6

26. 6.22×10^5

Check your answers on page 125.

27. $.26 \times 10^7$

28. 14.3×10^6

MATH AT WORK

1. Copy Clerk   Using a photocopier, Martha is reducing a document to .75 of its original size. The original document is 8.5 inches by 11 inches. How large will the copy be?

2. Mason   A customer asks Brenda to build a rectangular patio 8.33 feet long by 14.5 feet wide. What is the area of the patio in square feet?

3. Concrete Contractor   Devon is pouring a concrete sidewalk 3.5 feet wide and 16.5 feet long. What is the area of the concrete walk in square feet?

4. Truck Driver   Julie, the truck driver, has a map with a scale of 2 inches per mile. It is 7 inches from 3rd Street to 43rd Street, according to Julie's map. What is the distance in miles?

5. Food Server   Maybelle works in a delicatessen. A customer asks for 3.5 pounds of pastrami broken up into three packages. The first package is 0.88 pounds, the second is 1.3 pounds. How big is the third package?

6. Food Server   If pastrami cost $2.79 per pound, how much should Maybelle charge for 3.5 pounds of pastrami? Round off your answer to the nearest cent.

7. Line Worker Julian earns $8.40 per hour assembling starters. When he works overtime, he gets paid at 1.5 times his regular rate. How many dollars per hour does Julian earn when he works overtime?

8. Line Worker In one week, Julian worked 46 hours. Six of these hours counted as overtime. At the wages described in the previous question, how much was Julian's gross pay (before deductions) for the week?

9. Copy Clerk Doris makes a copy of a customer's drawing that is 1.5 times the length and width of the original. The original drawing is 6.75 centimeters wide by 7.5 centimeters long. How long and wide is the copy?

10. Copy Clerk Doris is asked to cover the enlargement she made in the previous question with plastic. Plastic overlay is sold by the square centimeter. To the nearest whole centimeter, what is the area of the enlargement?

11. Copy Clerk The plastic covering Doris uses costs .4¢ ($ .004) per square centimeter. Rounded to the nearest whole cent, how much should Doris charge for the plastic to cover the enlargement she made in the question above?

12. Landscaper John is bidding to do the landscaping on a block of duplexes. Each duplex has three flower beds. One bed is 5.25 feet by 6 feet. There are also two beds 4.5 feet by 18 feet flanking the driveway. What is the total area of flower beds for each duplex?

13. Landscaper   John is bidding on 8 identical duplexes with flower beds like the ones described above. What is the total area of the flower beds?

14. Landscaper   John did a similar job for $13.36 per square foot. If he bids the same amount for this job, what will his bid be? Give your answer to the nearest hundred dollars.

15. Truck Driver   Taylor delivered 3.64 tons of sand to a cement plant. There are 2,000 pounds in a ton. How many pounds of sand did Taylor deliver?

16. Plumber   Valerie bought 12.5 feet of $\frac{1}{4}$-inch plastic pipe and 46.5 feet of $\frac{3}{4}$-inch plastic pipe. The $\frac{1}{4}$-inch pipe was $ .48 per foot and the $\frac{3}{4}$-inch pipe was $1.08 per foot. How much did she spend in all?

17. Food Server   Mark has 4.25 gallons of cola syrup. There are 16 cups in a gallon. How many cups of syrup does Mark have?

18. Photographer   A customer brings a 4-inch-by -5-inch photo to Bob's studio. She wants it reduced by half, and then wants the copy reduced by half again. The size of the second copy will be what fraction of the size of the original? Express your answer as a decimal.

19. Painter Paul finds that he used 7 gallons of paint to paint a house. The paint cost $13.87 per gallon. How much did Paul spend on paint?

20. Painter Paul discovers that he can buy a 10-gallon can of his favorite paint for $129.98. Normally, the paint costs $13.87 per gallon. How much can Paul save by buying the ten-gallon can?

21. Computer Technician Jose is replacing a modem capable of transmitting 1.728×10^6 bits of information per minute. How much is 1.728×10^6?

22. Hairstylist Meredith, the hairstylist, wants to send out brochures to her customers announcing that she is changing beauty shops. How much will it cost her to mail 100 brochures at $ .32 per stamp?

23. Landscaper John is laying sod in an 80-feet-by-100-feet back yard. There are a 14.75-feet-by-22.5-feet swimming pool and two 34-feet-by-12- feet flower beds already established. How much sod will John need to buy?

24. Landscaper John rounds his estimate of the yard area to 6,900 square feet. If sod costs $ .79 for a 3-square-foot piece, how much will John spend on sod to do the job described above?

Check your answers
on page 126.

CHAPTER 4

Division with Decimals

LESSON 16   Dividing Decimals

Wanda bought 87.6 acres of land to develop into a business complex. She wants to divide it into equal sections to build 3 office buildings. Wanda divides to find how many acres each section will be.

Total Acres = 87.6

29.2	29.2	29.2

$$
\begin{array}{r}
29.2 \\
3\overline{)87.6} \\
-6 \\
\hline
27 \\
-27 \\
\hline
06 \\
-6 \\
\hline
0
\end{array}
$$

The illustration above shows how Wanda solves the problem to find how many acres will be in each section. This procedure is the same as dividing whole numbers, but the decimal point in the quotient is directly above the decimal point in the dividend.

Dividing Decimals by Whole Numbers

Wanda has built the first office building. Each office is 980.6 square feet. One tenant wants Wanda to divide an office into 4 equal rooms. How many square yards will each room be?

EXAMPLE 1

Divide 98.4 ÷ 3 = ?

Step 1	Step 2	Step 3	Step 4	Step 5	Step 6
$4\overline{)980.6}$	$\begin{array}{r}2.\\4\overline{)980.6}\\-8\\\hline 1\end{array}$	$\begin{array}{r}24.\\4\overline{)980.6}\\-8\\\hline 18\\-16\\\hline 2\end{array}$	$\begin{array}{r}245.\\4\overline{)980.6}\\-8\\\hline 18\\-16\\\hline 20\\-20\\\hline 0\end{array}$	$\begin{array}{r}245.1\\4\overline{)980.6}\\-8\\\hline 18\\-16\\\hline 20\\-20\\\hline 06\\-4\\\hline 2\end{array}$	$\begin{array}{r}245.15\\4\overline{)980.60}\\-8\\\hline 18\\-16\\\hline 20\\-20\\\hline 06\\-4\\\hline 20\\-20\\\hline 0\end{array}$

Step 1   Set up the problem. Place the decimal point in the correct position in the **dividend**. Set a decimal point directly above it in the **quotient**.

Step 2 Divide the hundreds: $9 \div 4 = 2$. Write a 2 in the tens place of the quotient. Multiply to check: $2 \times 4 = 8$. Subtract to find the remainder: $9 - 8 = 1$.

Step 3 Set the value in the tens place, 8, alongside the remainder, 1. Divide: $18 \div 4 = 4$. Write a 4 in the tens place of the quotient. Multiply to check: $4 \times 4 = 16$. Subtract to find the remainder: $18 - 16 = 2$.

Step 4 Set the value in the ones place, 0, alongside the remainder, 2. Divide the ones: $20 \div 4 = 5$. Write a 5 in the ones place of the quotient. Multiply to check: $5 \times 4 = 20$. Subtract to find the remainder: $20 - 20 = 0$.

Step 5 Set the value in the tenths place, 6, alongside the remainder, 0. Divide the ones: $6 \div 4 = 1$. Write a 1 in the tenths place of the quotient. Multiply to check: $1 \times 4 = 4$. Subtract to find the remainder: $6 - 4 = 2$.

Step 6 Write a 0 in the hundredths place of the dividend. Remember, extending the number with a 0 in a decimal column does not change the value of the number. Set the value in the hundredths place, 0, alongside the remainder, 2. Divide: $20 \div 4 = 5$. Write a 5 in the hundredths place of the quotient. Multiply to check: $5 \times 4 = 20$. Subtract to find the remainder: $20 - 20 = 0$.

EXERCISE 16A

Set up each example. Divide.

1. $22.4 \div 7 = ?$

2. $46.5 \div 6 = ?$

3. $32.64 \div 8 = ?$

4. $409.68 \div 15 = ?$

APPLICATION

5. Katherine teaches a pottery class. She has a box of clay that weighs 21.6 pounds. She needs to divide it equally among her 12 students. How many pounds of clay will each student get?

Check your answers on page 127.

Dividing Whole Numbers

Extending the division process by adding decimal places gives you another way to express remainders when you divide whole numbers.

Wanda buys more land to build a storage unit facility. One of the buildings will be 58 yards long. She wants to divide the building into 20 equal units. How many yards long will each unit be?

EXAMPLE 2

Divide 58 ÷ 20 = ?

$$
\begin{array}{r}
. \\
20\overline{)58.0}
\end{array}
\qquad
\begin{array}{r}
2. \\
20\overline{)58.0} \\
-40 \\
\hline
18
\end{array}
\qquad
\begin{array}{r}
2.9 \\
20\overline{)58.0} \\
-40 \\
\hline
180 \\
-180 \\
\hline
0
\end{array}
$$

   Step 1   Step 2   Step 3

Step 1   Set up the problem. Convert 58 into a decimal number by adding a decimal point after the ones column. Again, extending the number with a 0 in a decimal column does not change the value of the number. Write a 0 in the tenths column. Write a decimal point in the quotient so it is directly above the decimal point in the dividend.

Step 2   The tens cannot be divided. Group them with the ones. Divide the ones: $58 \div 20 = 2$. Write a 2 in the ones column of the quotient. Multiply to check: $2 \times 20 = 40$. Subtract to find the remainder: $58 - 40 = 18$. Write the 1 under the tens column. Write the 8 under the ones column.

Step 3   Set the value in the tenths place, 0, alongside the remainder, 18. Divide the tenths: $180 \div 20 = 9$. Write a 9 in the tenths column of the quotient. Multiply to check: $9 \times 20 = 180$. Subtract to find the remainder: $180 - 180 = 0$.

EXERCISE 16B

Set up each example. Divide until there are no remainders.

6. $83 \div 5 = ?$ **7.** $35 \div 50 = ?$

8. 318 ÷ 12 = ?   **9.** 711 ÷ 45 = ?

APPLICATION

10. Jermaine is building shelves in a cabinet that is 81 inches high. The owner wants 6 shelves evenly spaced. How far apart will Jermaine build the shelves?

Check your answers on page 127.

Add as many zeros as necessary to the end of a decimal number when dividing. It will not change the value of the number, and it helps you find the accurate quotient.	.2 = .20 $$\frac{2}{10} = \frac{20}{100}$$

USE WHAT YOU HAVE LEARNED

Set up each example. Divide.

1. 43.2 ÷ 9 = ?   **2.** 286.55 ÷ 11 = ?   **3.** 389.1 ÷ 15 = ?   **4.** 70 ÷ 8 = ?

APPLICATIONS

5. George is landscaping a yard. The customer wants to plant a hedge that will be 54.8 feet long. The plants are to be planted 2 feet apart. How many plants should George buy?

6. Elaine has 10 children in her preschool class. She has a 64-ounce bottle of juice to divide among them at snack. Elaine wants to give each child the same amount of juice and not have any left over. What is the smallest cup she can use? A 6, 8 or 12-ounce cup?

7. Dan is planning a new subdivision. After he allows for the land needed for roads and improvements, he has 28 acres left. He wants to put 40 lots in the subdivision. If each lot is the same size, how large will each lot be?

8. Sal owns a cleaning company. Three employees went with him to clean a house for a builder. Sam charges the builder $665 for the job. He keeps $75 for supplies and expenses. He divides the rest of the money 4 ways so that each worker will earn equal pay. How much will each worker earn?

9. Tim is delivering a 74-inch sofa. The customer wants it placed in the middle of a 171-inch wall. How many inches will be on each side of the sofa?

10. A case of 24 drinks costs Jane $3.60. She wants to sell them at her concession stand so that she will make a 30¢ profit on each drink. How much should Jane charge for each drink?

Check your answers on page 127.

LESSON 17 Decimal Remainders

Words to KNOW

Repeating decimal is a key word. It means that no matter how many zeros you add to the number to divide, there will always be a remainder.

Rounding is another key word. When you can not divide a decimal evenly, the number in the thousandths place is used to round to the nearest hundredths, unless directed otherwise. If the number in the thousandths place is 5 or higher, make the number in the hundredths place one number higher. If the number in the thousandths place is 4 or less, do not change the number in the hundredths place.

Pete works in the advertising department for a newspaper company. A three-line ad costs $18 and runs for one week. A customer wants to run an ad for one day only. Pete divides 7 into 18 and finds that the quotient is a **repeating decimal**.

```
Garage Sale  5-20 only
Furniture, clothes, toys
4508 Stone Dr.  8–5
```

```
        $2.568  or $2.57
    7)$18.000
      −14
        40
       −35
        50
       − 42
        60
```

The illustration above shows how Pete calculates the cost of running an ad for one day. When dividing, some numbers can never be divided equally. There will always be a remainder. These decimals are called repeating.

Repeating Numbers in Quotients

A page in the advertising section of the newspaper has a text width of 12.5 inches. Pete sets up the print into 3 columns. How wide will each column be?

EXAMPLE 1

Divide 12.5 ÷ 3 = ?

```
        .                4.1              4.16             4.166            4.166
    3)12.5           3)12.5          3)12.50          3)12.500         3)12.500
                       −12              −12              −12              −12
                        05               05               05               05
                       − 3              − 3              − 3              − 3
                         2               20               20               20
                                        −18              −18              −18
                                          2               20               20
                                                         −18              −18
                                                           2                2
    Step 1          Step 2           Step 3           Step 4           Step 5
```

Step 1 Set up the problem. Place the decimal point in the correct position in the dividend. Place a decimal point directly above it in the quotient.

Step 2   Divide the whole numbers: $12 \div 3 = 4$. Write a 4 in the ones place of the quotient. Multiply to check: $4 \times 3 = 12$. Subtract to find the remainder: $12 - 12 = 0$. Set the value in the tenths place, 5, alongside the remainder, 0. Divide the tenths: $5 \div 3 = 1$. Write a 1 in the tenths place of the quotient. Multiply to check: $1 \times 3 = 3$. Subtract to find the remainder: $5 - 3 = 2$.

Step 3   Write a 0 in the hundredths place of the dividend. (Remember, extending the number with a 0 in a decimal place does not change the value of the number.) Set the value in the hundredths place, 0, alongside the remainder, 2. Divide the hundredths: $20 \div 3 = 6$. Write a 6 in the hundredths place of the quotient. Multiply to check: $6 \times 3 = 18$. Subtract to find the remainder: $20 - 18 = 2$.

Step 4   Write another 0 in the dividend, this time in the thousandths place. Set the value in the thousandths place, 0, alongside the remainder, 2. Divide the thousandths: $20 \div 3 = 6$. Write a 6 in the thousandths place of the quotient. Multiply to check: $6 \times 3 = 18$. Subtract to find the remainder: $20 - 18 = 2$.

Step 5   Notice, the remainder is the same as the previous remainder. Creating another zero will create another dividend of 20 and another remainder of 2. Once you recognize that a decimal is repeating, quit dividing and place a bar over the repeating numbers in the quotient.

EXERCISE 17A

Set up each example. Divide to the thousandths place.

1. $18.8 \div 6 = ?$ 2. $41 \div 9 = ?$

3. $95.1 \div 27 = ?$ 4. $914 \div 18 = ?$

APPLICATION

5. Vivian has 28 yards of fabric to make covers for 12 sofa cushions. How much fabric can she use on each cushion?

Check your answers on page 128.

Rounding Numbers in Quotients

Often, repeating decimals are **rounded**.

The text length of the newspaper is 15.5 inches. Pete is laying out the paper so he can place 6 ads in a column. How wide will long will each ad be?

EXAMPLE 2

Divide 15.5 ÷ 6 = ?

```
                    2.5           2.58          2.583          2.5̲8̲3̲
    6)15.5       6)15.5        6)15.50       6)15.500       6)15.500
                  −12           −12           −12            −12
                   35            35            35             35
                  −30           −30           −30            −30
                    5            50            50             50
                                −48           −48            −48
                                  2            20             20
                                                             −18
                                                               2
   Step 1       Step 2        Step 3        Step 4         Step 5
```

Step 1 Set up the problem. Place the decimal point in the correct position of the dividend. Place a decimal point directly above it in the quotient.

Step 2 Divide the whole numbers: 15 ÷ 6 = 2. Write a 2 in the ones place of the quotient. Multiply to check: 2 x 6 = 12. Subtract to find the remainder: 15 − 12 = 3. Set the value in the tenths place, 5, alongside the remainder, 3. Divide the tenths: 35 ÷ 6 = 5. Write a 5 in the tenths place of the quotient. Multiply to check: 5 × 6 = 30. Subtract to find the remainder: 35 − 30 = 5.

Step 3 Write a 0 in the hundredths place of the dividend. Set the value in the hundredths place, 0, alongside the remainder, 5. Divide the hundredths: 50 ÷ 6 = 8. Write an 8 in the hundredths place of the quotient. Multiply to check: 8 × 6 = 48. Subtract to find the remainder: 50 − 48 = 2.

Step 4 Write a 0 in the thousandths place of the dividend. Set the value in the thousandths place, 0, alongside the remainder, 2. Divide the thousandths: 20 ÷ 6 = 3. Write a 3 in the thousandths place of the quotient. Multiply to check: 3 × 6 = 18. Subtract to find the remainder: 20 − 18 = 2.

Step 5 Since the remainder is 2 again, creation of another 0 will result in a repeating decimal. Round the quotient to the nearest hundredth. Look at the 3 in the thousandths place. The number 3 is four or less, so the 8 in the hundredths place will not change. 2.6833 rounded to the nearest hundredth is 2.68.

EXERCISE 17B

Set up each example. Divide. Round to the hundredths place.

6. 42.6 ÷ 7 = ?

7. 53.4 ÷ 22 = ?

8. 75 ÷ 14 = ?

9. 581.8 ÷ 37 = ?

APPLICATION

Check your answers
on page 129.

10. Carol owns a candy shop. She has 65 pounds of hand-dipped chocolates to put equally into 32 boxes. How much will each box of candy weigh?

MATH TIP

As you add zeros to a decimal, if the remainder is the same in two successive divisions, then stop working the problem. The decimal is a repeating decimal.

USE WHAT YOU HAVE LEARNED

Set up each example. Divide. Round to the nearest hundredth.

1. 24.6 ÷ 7 = ?

2. 75 ÷ 9 = ?

3. 328 ÷ 27 = ?

4. 167.4 ÷ 16 = ?

APPLICATIONS

5. Elaine drives a cargo truck. She must drive a total 1,235 miles in 3 days to get to all of her stops. On an average, how many miles must she drive each day?

6. Neil is installing a lawn sprinkler system. He needs 139 feet of pipe. the pipes come in 8 foot lengths. How many pipes will Neil buy?

7. Beth mailed 35 questionnaires. It cost her a total of $13.48. How much did it cost to mail each questionnaire?

8. Jose is installing 13 recessed lights in an office building hallway that is 135 feet long. If he spaces the lights evenly and if he rounds the distance between them to the nearest whole foot, how far apart will he put the lights? Jose needs to center the lights in the hallway. How far from each end of the hallway will he install the lights? Draw a diagram to help yourself.

9. The hotel punch bowl holds 5.5 gallons of punch. Judy mixes 1 gallon of lemonade, .8 gallons of orange juice, and 1.2 gallons of carbonated drink to make the punch recipe. How many batches of punch recipe can Judy put into the bowl to fill it?

10. Pam is a distributor of hair care products. She is running a special on shampoo. She will sell a case of 12 bottles for $39.99. The regular price of the shampoo is $57.99 per case. How much will each bottle of shampoo cost on sale? How much does it cost at the regular price? How much will people save per bottle if they buy the shampoo on sale?

Check your answers on page 129.

LESSON 18   Zeros in the Dividend

Kyle wants to compute the gas mileage of his truck. The truck used 19 gallons of gas to go 380.6 miles. How many miles per gallon is Kyle's truck getting?

Dividing One or More Zeros in the Dividend

As with division of whole numbers with one or more zeros in the dividend, you can simplify a division problem involving decimals.

EXAMPLE 1

Divide 380.6 ÷ 19 = ?

$$
\begin{array}{r}
. \\
19\overline{)380.6}
\end{array}
\qquad
\begin{array}{r}
2\ . \\
19\overline{)380.6} \\
-38 \\
\hline
0
\end{array}
\qquad
\begin{array}{r}
20. \\
19\overline{)380.6} \\
-38 \\
\hline
00
\end{array}
\qquad
\begin{array}{r}
20.031 \\
19\overline{)380.600} \\
-38 \\
\hline
0060 \\
-57 \\
\hline
30 \\
-19 \\
\hline
11
\end{array}
\qquad
20.03
$$

Step 1   Step 2   Step 3   Step 4   Step 5

Step 1   Set up the problem. Place the decimal point in the correct position in the dividend. Place a decimal point directly above it in the quotient.

Step 2   Regroup the hundreds with the tens. Divide the tens: $38 \div 19 = 2$. Write a 2 in the tens column of the quotient. Multiply to check: $2 \times 19 = 38$. Subtract to find the remainder: $38 - 38 = 0$.

Step 3   Set the value in the dividend's ones place, 0, beside the remainder, 0. Since there is 0 remainder and there are 0 ones, write 0 in the ones place of the quotient.

Step 4   Set the value in the dividend's tenths place, 6, beside the remainder, 0. Since there are 0 groups of 24 in 6, write a 0 in the tenths place of the quotient. Write a 0 in the hundredths column of the dividend. Set the value in the hundredths place, 0, beside the remainder, 6. Regroup the tenths with the hundredths. Divide the hundredths: $60 \div 19 = 3$. Write a 3 in the hundredths place of the quotient. Multiply to check: $3 \times 19 = 57$. Subtract to find the remainder: $60 - 57 = 3$. Write a 0 in the thousandths place of the dividend. Set the value in the thousandths place, 0, beside the remainder, 3. Regroup the hundredths and the thousandths. Divide the thousandths: $30 \div 19 = 1$. Write a 1 in the thousandths column of the quotient. Multiply to check: $1 \times 19 = 19$. Subtract to find the remainder: $30 - 19 = 11$.

Step 5   The number continues to have remainders. The number in the hundredths column will stay the same after rounding.

EXERCISE 18A

Set up each example. Divide.

1. $90.54 \div 3 = ?$

2. $156.08 \div 4 = ?$

3. $720.36 \div 12 = ?$

4. $4,607.56 \div 15 = ?$

APPLICATION

Check your answers on page 131.

5. Nathan needs 1,806.3 cubic yards of concrete for an office building slab. Concrete trucks can hold 9 cubic yards of concrete. How many truck loads of concrete should Nathan order?

Dividing Decimals with Two or More Zeros

Kyle has 5 bags of grass seed totaling 480.02 pounds. If he uses 24 pounds of seed each day, how many days supply of grass seed does Kyle have?

EXAMPLE 2

Divide 480.02 ÷ 24 = ?

```
        .              20.            20.00           20.000
   24)480.02      24)480.02       24)480.02       24)480.020     20.00 or
                     -48             -48             -48         20 days
                     ----            -----           ------
                      00             0002            00020

     Step 1          Step 2          Step 3          Step 4         Step 5
```

Step 1   Set up the problem. Place the decimal point in the correct position in the dividend. Place a decimal point directly above it in the quotient.

Step 2   Regroup the hundreds with the tens. Divide the tens: $48 \div 24 = 2$. Write a 2 in the tens column of the quotient. Multiply to check: $2 \times 24 = 48$. Subtract to find the remainder: $48 - 48 = 0$. Set the value in the dividend's ones place, 0, beside the remainder, 0. Since there is 0 remainder and there are 0 ones, write a 0 in the ones place of the quotient.

Step 3 Set the value in the dividend's tenths place, 0, beside the remainder, 0. Since there is 0 remainder and there are 0 ones, write a 0 in the tenths place of the quotient. Set the value in the hundredths place, 2, beside the remainder, 0. Since there are 0 full groups of 24 in 2, write a 0 in the hundredths column of the quotient.

Step 4 Set a 0 in the thousandths column of the dividend. Since there are 0 full groups of 24 in 20, write 0 in the thousandths place of the quotient. The number continues to have remainders. Stop working the problem. The number in the hundredths column will stay the same after rounding.

Step 5 Since Kyle's question concerned the number of full days of grass seed that he had, round the number to the nearest whole number.

EXERCISE 18B

Set up each example. Divide.

6. 80.02 ÷ 5 = ?

7. 60.01 ÷ 2 = ?

8. 200.10 ÷ 10 = ?

9. 7,002.45 ÷ 14 = ?

APPLICATION

10. Van sells furniture. His store is offering a no interest payment plan for 12 months. With tax included, a customer buys $1,206.09 worth of furniture. How much does Van tell the customer to pay each month?

Check your answers on page 131.

MATH TIP

The number of zeros in a problem does not tell you how many zeros will be in the quotient. You must find the remainder from each step before writing the zero in the quotient.

USE WHAT YOU HAVE LEARNED

Divide.

1. 80.4 ÷ 8 = ?

2. 3,005.4 ÷ 6 = ?

3. 900.05 ÷ 15 = ?

4. 600,002.83 ÷ 20 = ?

APPLICATIONS

5. Lisa buys 200.76 quarts of juice to make punch for several parties she is catering. Her recipe calls for using gallons of juice. How many gallons of juice does Lisa have? (Hint: There are 4 quarts in a gallon.)

6. Josh is a warehouse distributor. He has 2,008 pounds of shrimp to divide equally and send to 10 stores. How much will Josh send to each store?

7. Charla has a contract with a major store to make 7 service calls per day to repair appliances. She earns a flat fee of $350 per day. One day it takes her 9 hours to finish 7 calls. Another day it takes her 5 hours to make the calls. What is Charla's hourly pay for each day?

8. Mona works an 8-hour day. She has 6 stops to make to restock snack racks in stores. Including driving time, what is the most amount of time she can spend on each stop? (Hint: There are 60 minutes in an hour.)

9. Joy earned $100.95 of tips working as a waitress Thursday night. She had 10 customers that night. What was her average tip rate that night?

10. Joel pays $12,025.45 for a car for his car rental company. He plans on paying an additional $475 for fees and maintenance during the year. He will charge $125 for a one week rental. How many times must Joel rent out the car before he can begin making a profit?

Check your answers on page 132.

LESSON 19 Dividing by Decimals

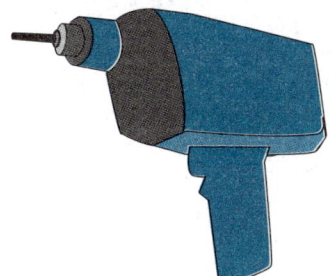

Danny is a custom home builder. He is calculating the bid for a house based on the blueprints. There is 97.5 linear feet of wall in the kitchen. If Danny places the studs on 1.3 foot centers, how many studs will he need?

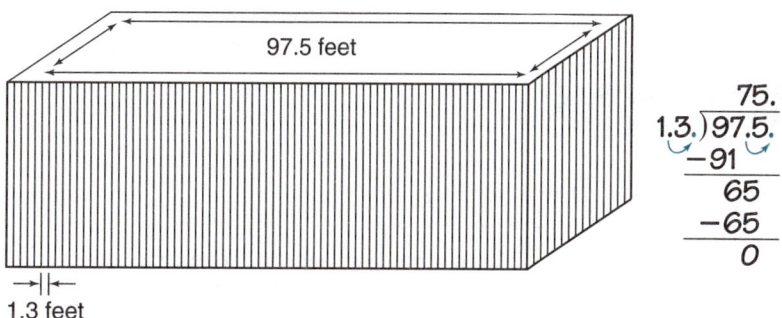

97.5 feet

1.3 feet

$$\begin{array}{r} 75. \\ 1.3\overline{)97.5.} \\ -91 \\ \hline 65 \\ -65 \\ \hline 0 \end{array}$$

Decimal Points in the Dividend and Divisor

The illustration above shows how Danny divides to compute the number of studs he will need to order. Notice that before he divided, Danny converted his decimal divisor into a whole number. When the divisor contains a decimal point, move the decimal point to the right to make the divisor a whole number. Move the decimal point in the dividend to the right the same number of places.

An outside shed has 27.2 linear feet of wall. If the studs have 1.6 foot centers, how many studs will Danny need?

EXAMPLE 1

Divide 27.2 ÷ 1.6 = ?

$$1.6\overline{)27.2} \qquad 16.\overline{)272.} \qquad \begin{array}{r} 1 \\ 16.\overline{)272.} \\ -16 \\ \hline 11 \end{array} \qquad \begin{array}{r} 17. \\ 16.\overline{)272.} \\ -16 \\ \hline 1\,12 \\ -1\,12 \\ \hline 0 \end{array}$$

Step 1   Step 2   Step 3   Step 4

Step 1   Set up the problem. Place the decimal point in the correct position in the dividend and divisor. Do not write the decimal point in the quotient yet.

$$\text{divisor}\overline{)\text{dividend}}^{\text{quotient}}$$

Step 2   Move the decimal point in the divisor one place to the right to make it a whole number. Move the decimal point in the dividend to the right the same number of places. Now, set a decimal point in the quotient so it is directly above the one in the dividend.

Step 3 Regroup the hundreds and tens places. Divide the tens: $27 \div 16 = 1$. Write a 1 in the tens place. Multiply to check: $1 \times 16 = 16$. Subtract to find the remainder: $27 - 16 = 1$.

Step 4 Set the number in the dividend's ones place, 2, aside the remainder, 11. Regroup the 11 tens with the 2 ones. Divide the ones: $112 \div 16 = 7$. Write a 7 in the quotient's ones place. Multiply to check: $7 \times 16 = 112$. Subtract to find the remainder: $112 - 112 = 0$.

EXERCISE 19A

Set up each example. Divide.

1. $27.2 \div .4 = ?$

2. $85.41 \div 3.9 = ?$

3. $90.44 \div .17 = ?$

4. $9.708 \div .06 = ?$

APPLICATION

Check your answers on page 133.

5. Meryl has 35.75 yards of fabric to make costumes that need 3.25 yards each. How many costumes can Meryl make?

Dividing Decimals into Whole Numbers

There are 42 square feet of tile space in the laundry room. The customer chooses an 8-inch tile to put in the room. Danny divides 64 square inches (the number of square inches in an 8 inch × 8 inch tile) by 144 square inches (the number of square inches in a square foot) to find that an 8-inch tile is .44 square feet. Danny then divides the area of the floor by .44 to determine how much tile to order. How much tile will Danny order?

EXAMPLE 2

Divide 42 ÷ .44 = ?

Step 1 Set up the problem. Place the decimal point in the correct position in the dividend and divisor. Do not write the decimal point. in the quotient yet.

$$44\overline{)42.}$$

Step 2 Move the decimal point in the divisor two places to the right to make it a whole number. Move the decimal point in the dividend to the right the same number of places. Write two zeros as place holders in the dividend. Place a decimal point in the quotient so it is directly above the decimal point in the dividend.

$$44.\overline{)4200.}$$

Step 3 Regroup the thousands, hundreds and tens columns. Divide the tens: $420 \div 44 = 9$. Write a 9 in the quotient's tens column. Multiply to check: $9 \times 44 = 396$. Subtract to find the remainder: $420 - 396 = 24$. Set the value in the dividend's ones place, 0, beside the remainder, (24). Regroup the tens and ones. Divide the ones: $240 \div 44 = 5$. Write 5 in the quotient's ones place. Multiply to check: $5 \times 44 = 220$. Subtract to find the remainder: $240 - 220 = 20$.

$$
\begin{array}{r}
95. \\
44.\overline{)4200.} \\
-396 \\
\hline
240 \\
-220 \\
\hline
20
\end{array}
$$

Step 4 Write a zero in the dividend's tenths place. Set the value in the dividend's tenths place (0) beside the remainder (20). Regroup the ones and tenths. Divide the tenths column: $200 \div 44 = 4$ Multiply to check: $4 \times 44 = 176$. Subtract to find the remainder. $200 - 176 = 24$.

$$
\begin{array}{r}
95.4 \\
44.\overline{)4200.0} \\
-396 \\
\hline
240 \\
-220 \\
\hline
200 \\
-176 \\
\hline
24
\end{array}
$$

Step 5 Since Danny is estimating whole tiles, he rounds his answer to the next larger whole number (even though 95.4 is nearer 95 than 96).

96

EXERCISE 19B

Set up each example. Divide.

6. $54 \div .3 = ?$

7. $78 \div 2.6 = ?$

8. $330.4 \div .14 = ?$

9. $102 \div 2.04 = ?$

APPLICATION

Check your answers on page 134.

10. Gail is preparing breakfast for the residents of the nursing home. There are 21 ounces of cereal in a box. A serving size is 1.4 ounces. How many servings will Gail get from one box?

After changing the decimal divisor in to a whole number, write as many zeros as you need in the dividend as place holders.

USE WHAT YOU HAVE LEARNED

Set up each example. Divide.

1. 13.6 ÷ .4 = ?   **2.** 67.9 ÷ 1.94 = ?   **3.** 288 ÷ 1.8 = ?   **4.** 69.94 ÷ 5.2 = ?

APPLICATIONS

5. John is to order an 8-inch tile for a room that is 35.2 square feet. An 8-inch tile is .44 square feet. How much tile will John order?

6. Chandra makes bows at the craft store. She needs 4.5 yards to make a small bow. One bolt of ribbon holds 50 yards. How many bows can she make from one bolt?

7. Gas costs $1.13 a gallon. How many gallons of gas can Kate buy with $17.00?

8. Janice assembles craft kits in her home. It takes her 3.33 minutes per kit. How many kits can she put together in one hour? If Janice makes 45¢ per kit, how much does she make each hour? (Hint: There are 60 minutes in one hour.)

9. Mike assembles wires on circuit boards. Each board requires 12.4 centimeters of wire. There are 25.5 meters of wire on a spool. How many circuit boards can Mike assemble with one spool? (Hint: There are 100 centimeters in a meter.)

10. Greg needs 820 square feet of gray bricks. The brick company has 3,861 of them. Are there enough bricks for Greg to finish the job? If so, how many are left over? If not, how many more bricks does Greg need? (Hint: There are 5.5 bricks in a square foot.)

Check your answers
on page 134.

LESSON 20   Converting Fractions to Decimals

Alice works in a fabric store. A customer is making a quilt and asks Alice to cut $\frac{1}{4}$-yard pieces of different fabrics. To write the sales ticket, Alice must convert the fraction to a decimal. Alice divides the denominator into the numerator to find what decimal to write on the ticket.

Fabric Shop	
Yards	
1/4 yd.	.25
1/4 yd.	.25

$$
\begin{array}{r}
.25 \\
4\overline{)1.00} \\
-8 \\
\hline
20 \\
-20 \\
\hline
0
\end{array}
$$

The problem above shows how Alice writes the fraction as a decimal. The denominator of the fraction becomes the divisor. The numerator becomes the dividend.

Words to KNOW

The **numerator** is the top number in a fraction.
The **denominator** is the bottom answer in a fraction.

$$\frac{\text{numerator}}{\text{denominator}}$$

The **divisor** is the number in a division problem that you are dividing by.
The **dividend** is the number being divided.
The **quotient** is the answer.

$$\text{divisor}\overline{)\text{dividend}}^{\,\text{quotient}}$$

When you convert fractions to decimals, divide.
Use the numerator of the fraction as the dividend. Use the denominator as the divisor.
The decimal equivalent is quotient.

$$\text{denominator}\overline{)\text{numerator}}^{\,\text{decimal}}$$

Dividing Fractions

Alice cuts $\frac{7}{8}$ of a yard of ribbon for a customer. How can she write the fraction as a decimal on the ticket?

EXAMPLE 1

Convert $\dfrac{7}{8}$ to a decimal. Divide $7 \div 8 = ?$

Step 1   Set up the problem. Write the 7 as the dividend. Write a decimal point after the 7 to make it a decimal. Write the 8 as the divisor. Write a decimal point in the quotient directly above the one in the dividend.

Step 2 Write a 0 in the tenths column. Regroup the ones and tenths. Divide the tenths: $70 \div 8 = 8$. Write an 8 in the tenths column of the quotient. Multiply to check: $8 \times 8 = 64$. Subtract to find the remainder: $70 - 64 = 6$.

```
   .8
8)7.0
  -64
    6
```

Step 3 Write a 0 in the hundredths column. Bring down the 0 hundredths. Regroup the tenths and hundredths. Divide the hundredths: $60 \div 8 = 7$. Write a 7 in the hundredths column of the quotient. Multiply to check: $7 \times 8 = 56$. Subtract to find the remainder: $60 - 56 = 4$.

```
   .87
8)7.00
  -64
    60
   -56
     4
```

Step 4 Write a 0 in the thousandths column. Bring down the 0 thousandths. Regroup the hundredths and thousandths. Divide the thousandths: $40 \div 8 = 5$. Write a 5 in the thousandths column of the quotient. Multiply to check: $5 \times 8 = 40$. Subtract to find the remainder: $40 - 40 = 0$.

```
   .875
8)7.000
  -64
    60
   -56
     40
    -40
      0
```

Step 5 Round the quotient to the nearest hundredth.

.88

EXERCISE 20

Convert each fraction to a decimal. If necessary, round to the nearest hundredth.

1. $\dfrac{1}{3} = ?$

2. $\dfrac{2}{5} = ?$

3. $\dfrac{5}{6} = ?$

4. $\dfrac{11}{16} = ?$

APPLICATION

5. Mark is delivering a refrigerator. The directions say to go $\frac{5}{8}$ of a mile before turning right. How will Mark rename the fraction as a decimal so he can use his odometer to help him?

Check your answers on page 135.

USE WHAT YOU HAVE LEARNED

Convert each fraction to a decimal. If necessary, round to the nearest hundredth.

1. $\dfrac{4}{5} = ?$

2. $\dfrac{3}{7} = ?$

3. $6\dfrac{2}{6} = ?$

4. $12\dfrac{5}{9} = ?$

APPLICATIONS

5. Tamara works in a deli. A customer asks for $\frac{3}{4}$ pound of salami. What decimal weight will Tamara write on the price tag?

6. Nathan works $7\frac{2}{3}$ hours on Monday. How will he write the number as a decimal on his time card? Round the answer to the nearest hundredth.

7. Alice cut a piece of fabric that is $1\frac{3}{4}$ yards long. The customer decide to get another $\frac{1}{3}$ of a yard to make a matching headband. How will Alice write the total yardage in decimal form on the ticket?

8. Alex is screwing together two boards that are 1 inch thick and 2.75 inches thick. He has a $3\frac{1}{2}$ inch screw. Will the screw go through both boards? If the screw is too short, by how much? If the screw goes through, how much of the screw will be exposed?

9. Ellen drives a taxi. She charges $1.25 for each $\frac{1}{4}$ mile. How much will she charge if she drives a passenger $3\frac{1}{4}$ miles?

10. Thomas owns a meat market. A customer asks that a 21.06 pound ribeye roast be cut into $2\frac{1}{2}$ pound steaks. Any left over should be ground into hamburger. How many steaks can Thomas cut? How much will be ground into hamburger?

Check your answers on page 135.

CHAPTER 4 Summary

When dividing a decimal or mixed decimal by a whole number, begin by placing a decimal point in the quotient above the decimal point in the dividend. Then divide. Zeros added to the dividend allow you to continue dividing remainders.

EXERCISE A

Divide.

1. $25.6 \div 8 =$

2. $159.9 \div 13 =$

3. $333.5 \div 23 =$

4. $99.75 \div 7 =$

Check your answers on page 137.

Repeating Decimals

Often, decimal remainders repeat. No matter how many zeros you add to the end of the dividend, the quotient never comes out even. You can indicate a repeating decimal by drawing a bar drawn over the repeating portion of the quotient. Or, you can round the decimal. Rounding to the hundredths place is adequate in many situations.

EXERCISE B

Divide the following. Indicate repeating decimals with a bar. Then round the quotient to the nearest hundredth.

5. $41.23 \div 9 =$ _____ rounded to nearest hundred

6. $443.5 \div 6 =$ _____ rounded to nearest hundred

Check your answers on page 137.

Dividing by Decimals

When a decimal appears as part to the divisor move the decimal to the right until the divisor becomes a whole number. Move the decimal in the dividend an equal number of places. Divide.

EXERCISE C

Check your answers on page 137.

Divide.

7. $46 \div .23 =$ **8.** $48.3 \div 2.5 =$ **9.** $9 \div .045 =$

Converting Fractions into Decimals.

Convert fractions into decimals by dividing the numerator by the denominator.

EXERCISE D

Check your answers on page 138.

Convert the following common fractions into decimal fractions. Place a bar over the repeating portion of decimals.

10. $\dfrac{3}{8} =$ **11.** $\dfrac{2}{3} =$ **12.** $\dfrac{5}{12} =$

MATH AT WORK

1. **Nurse** Bruno is a nurse. His patient's heart beats 42 times in 0.5 minute. What is her heart rate, in beats per minute?

2. **Cook** Carla is cooking barbecue beef for school lunches. The recipe makes 6 servings, but Carla needs to make 150 servings. The recipe calls for 2.5 pounds of meat. How much meat should Carla use to make 150 servings of stew?

3. **Sales Clerk** Glenda sells appliances. A television was marked down to 0.75 its regular price for a sale. Its sale price is $156. What is the regular price of the television?

4. **Carpet Layer** Bill must carpet a room that is 12.3 feet × 10.6 feet. He knows area is found by multiplying length times width. Carpet is sold by the yard. There are 9 square feet in 1 square yard. To the nearest tenth of a square yard, how many square yards of carpet does Bill need?

5. **Contractor** A set of blueprints is drawn so that 1.5 inches on the drawing is equal to 1 foot in the building it represents. A wall is 12 inches long on the blueprints. How many feet long is the actual wall?

6. **Contractor** On another set of drawings, 1.25 inches on the drawing is equal to 1 foot in the building it represents. A handicap ramp 20 feet long would appear how long on the blueprint?

7. Butcher   There are 16 ounces in 1 pound. How many pounds is 62-ounce steak?

8. Truck Driver   Julie is a truck driver. She is going to drive 250 miles at an average speed of 40 miles per hour. How long will it take her to reach his destination?

9. Nurse   Millie is a nurses' aide. One of his patients usually gets 3.5 ounces of vitamin supplement each day. Today the doctor tells Millie to give the patient a quarter of his usual amount of supplement. How much vitamin supplement does Millie's patient get today?

10. Designer   Georgia is making a scale drawing of a bicycle. Georgia's drawing is .125 the actual size of the bike. The bike in Georgia's drawing is 3.25 inches tall. How tall is the actual bike?

11. Food Service   At Mark's Burger Palace, a medium drink contains 1.25 cups of soda. How many medium sodas can Mark get from 1 gallon of soda? One gallon is 16 cups.

12. Truck Driver   At an average speed of 58 miles per hour, how far could Julie drive in 15 minutes?

MATH AT WORK

13. **Accountant**   Bill is adding an office to his house. There are 304 square feet of wall space. A piece of sheet rock covers 32 square feet. How many pieces of sheet rock does Bill need to buy?

14. **Barn Manager**   Erika is a barn manager. A horse eats 7.5 pounds of oats each day. The oats are sold in 100 pound bags. For how long will one bag feed one horse?

15. **Developer**   Juanita owns 80.96 acres of land. She wants to divide it into 8 lots. If the lots are of equal size, how large will each lot be?

16. **Phone**   Operator Amy works part time for a temporary service for $6.75 an hour. She answers phones at one office for $4\frac{3}{4}$ hours in the morning. How much money does Amy earn on the assignment?

17. **Craftsman**   John is making screens for windows that are 4.8 feet tall. He has a 150 foot roll of screen material. How many screens can he make?

18. **Salesperson**   Zeke is paying $409 for insurance on a company car. He wants to make 4 payments over the course of the year. He has to pay an additional $2 handling fee on each installment. How much will Zeke pay for his car insurance?

19. Baker   Alicia owns a bakery. She orders bags of flour that weigh 20.66 kilograms. Her bread recipe calls for 4.1 kilograms. How many batches of bread dough can Alicia make from one bag?

20. Plumber   Charles is a plumber. He estimates that it will take him 9.08 hours to install 3 toilets. How long will it take to install each one?

21. Dog Groomer   It takes Elida 1.6 hours to groom a dog. How many dogs can she groom in an 8 hour day?

22. Food Service   Clara manages the school cafeteria. There are 85.81 ounces of peaches in one can. A serving size of peaches is $4\frac{1}{4}$ ounces. How many servings can Clara prepare from one can? If she has 138 children to feed, then how many cans will she need?

23. Carpenter   Mason is building the dressing room for a store. The room is 12.5 feet wide and 30 feet long. The store wants each dressing room to be 3.75 feet squared with a row of rooms along each side of the wall. How wide will the center aisle be? How many dressing rooms can Mason build on each side? How many rooms total will there be?

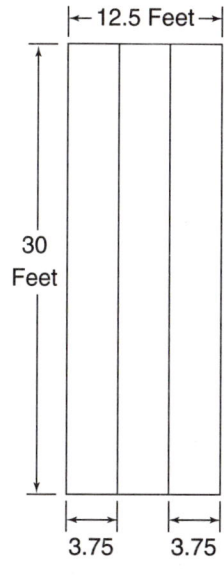

24. Retail Clerk   Wendy writes up a layaway purchase that totals $91.19. The customer makes a deposit of $9.11. The balance is to be paid in equal monthly payments for 3 months. How much does Wendy tell the customer to pay each month?

Check your answers on page 138.

CHAPTER 1 Introduction to Decimals

LESSON 1 Decimals and Fractions   **pages 1–3**

EXERCISE 1

1. This chart is completed by finding the number of pockets on the Fraction/Decimal Equivalency Chart and reading to the right to find the simplest fraction and the decimal value.

Date	Worker's Name	# Pockets	Fraction	Decimal
8/25/96	1. Marta	71	5/7	.71
	2. Elmer	57	4/7	.57
	3. Bill	78	7/9	.78
	4. Susan	80	4/5	.80
	5. Jasmina	66	2/3	.66

2. Yolanda needs 5 rolls of Tri-X film and 4 rolls of color film. Look up .5 on the Fraction/Decimal Equivalency Chart: $5 = \frac{1}{2}$. 10 rolls of film $\times \frac{1}{2} = 5$ rolls. Look up .4 on the Fraction/Decimal Equivalency Chart: $4 = \frac{2}{5}$. 10 rolls of film $\times \frac{2}{5} = 4$ rolls.

USE WHAT YOU HAVE LEARNED

1. This chart is filled in by finding the number given on the Fraction/Decimal Equivalency Chart and reading to the left or right to find the missing values.

Date	Worker's Name	# Pockets	Fraction	Decimal
8/26/96	6. Marta	42	3/7	.42
	7. Elmer	38	3/8	.38
	8. Bill	44	4/9	.44
	9. Susan	56	5/7	.56
	10. Jasmina	89	8/9	.89

2. Find the fraction equivalent: .50 yards $= \frac{1}{2}$ yard.
   1 yard = 36 inches
   Multiply 36 inches by the fraction: 36 inches $\times \frac{1}{2} = 18$ inches

3. Find the decimal equivalency of $\frac{1}{5}$ on the chart: $\frac{1}{5} = .20$
   This is the answer because odometers record mileage in decimals.

4. Find the fraction equivalent of .50 gallons: $.50 = \frac{1}{2}$.
   Multiply 128 ounces by $\frac{1}{2} = 64$ ounces of orange juice.
   Find the fraction equivalent of .25: $.25 = \frac{1}{4}$.
   Multiply 128 ounces by $\frac{1}{4} = 32$ ounces of pineapple juice.

Multiply 128 ounces by $\frac{1}{4} = 32$ ounces of coconut milk.

Add   64 ounces of orange juice
            32 ounces of pineapple juice
       +32 ounces of coconut milk
         128 ounces is the total amount this recipe will make.

5. Multiply the capacity of the tank by the miles per gallon.
10 gallons × 30 miles per gallon = 300 miles per tank.

Find the fraction equivalent of .4: $.4 = \frac{2}{5}$.

Multiply the total miles per tank by $\frac{2}{5}$: $300 \times \frac{2}{5} = 120$ miles.

6. Multiply the capacity of the tank by the miles per gallon.
10 gallons × 30 miles to the gallon = 300 miles per tank.
Divide the miles driven by the total miles per tank: $60 \div 300 = \frac{1}{5}$.

Find the decimal equivalent of $\frac{1}{5}$ on the chart: $\frac{1}{5} = .20$.

7. Convert the number of calls made into a fraction of the total $\frac{60}{100}$.

Reduce this to its lowest terms: $\frac{60}{100} = \frac{6}{10} = \frac{3}{5}$.

Find the decimal equivalent of $\frac{3}{5}$ on the chart: $\frac{3}{5} = .60$.

LESSON 2 Decimal Place Value and Mixed Decimals   pages 4–7

EXERCISE 2A

1.

Steak #	Weight	Use words to write the weight of each steak.
1	1.1	One and one tenth
2	1.05	One and five hundredths
3	1.005	One and five thousandths
4	0.999	Nine hundred ninety-nine thousandths
5	0.955	Nine hundred fifty-five thousandths
6	1.9	One and nine tenths
7	1.000	One
8	0.855	Eight hundred fifty-five thousandths
9	0.75	Seventy-five hundreths
10	0.935	Nine hundred thirty-five thousandths

EXERCISE 2B

2.

Date	Employee	Time In	Time Out	Hours	Decimal
8/24/96	Smith, J.W.	8:30 a.m.	5:00 p.m.	8 1/2	8.50
	Perez, Al	8:00 a.m.	4:15 p.m.	8 1/4	8.25
	Black, Ann	8:30 a.m.	2:45 p.m.	6 1/4	6.25
	Ortiz, Anna	8:00 a.m.	6:00 p.m.	10	10
	Jones, Pat	8:30 a.m.	4:45 p.m.	8 3/4	8.75
	Alto, Eddie	8:15 a.m.	7:00 p.m.	10 3/4	10.75

1.

Write each decimal number in words.
two hundred one and fifty hundredths (or five tenths) hours
thirty-three and three tenths acres
one thousand, twenty and ninety-seven hundredths dollars
eighty and four hundredths pounds
ten and four hundred forty-five thousandths gallons

2. **a.** $10.49   **b.** 500.05   **c.** .999   **d.** .6   **e.** .59

3. **b.** 0.005   **c.** 0.094   **e.** 8.099   have 0 in the tenths place. The tenths place is the first place to the right of the decimal point.

4. **a.** 4.303   **b.** 0.005   have 0 in the hundredths place. The hundredths place is the second place to the right of the decimal point.

5. **c.** 0.990   **d.** 4.050   **e.** 8.110   have 0 in the thousandths place. The thousandths place is the third place to the right of the decimal point.

6. No, Jack does not have enough money. $5\frac{1}{2}$ dollars is $5.50, and Jack has only $5.25.

7. Jane's package weighs four and eight hundred twenty-five thousandths pounds. "And" signifies the position of the decimal point.

8.

Fred's Shopping List		
Catalog Item	Price	W/M/D
Staples	$ 0.99	D
Pens	$ 1.00	W
Paper	$ 3.95	M
Pencil Sharpener	$ 10.98	M
File Cabinet	$ 39.95	M

9. Two tenths is the written in the form of .2.

LESSON 3 Converting Decimals to Fractions   pages 8–10

One digit decimals represent tenths.

	decimal	fraction	simplified		decimal	fraction	simplified
1.	.3	$\frac{3}{10}$	$\frac{3}{10}$	2.	.5	$\frac{5}{10}$	$\frac{1}{2}$
3.	.1	$\frac{1}{10}$	$\frac{1}{10}$	4.	.6	$\frac{6}{10}$	$\frac{3}{5}$
5.	.8	$\frac{8}{10}$	$\frac{4}{5}$				

Two digit decimal numbers represent hundredths.

	decimal	fraction	simplified		decimal	fraction	simplified
6.	.25	$\frac{25}{100}$	$\frac{1}{4}$	7.	.33	$\frac{33}{100}$	$\frac{1}{3}$
8.	.57	$\frac{57}{100}$	$\frac{57}{100}$	9.	.70	$\frac{70}{100}$	$\frac{7}{10}$
10.	.75	$\frac{75}{100}$	$\frac{3}{4}$				

11. $\frac{7}{20}$ of the employees have taken no sick leave. $.35 = \frac{35}{100} = \frac{7}{20}$

EXERCISE 3B

	mixed decimal	mixed fraction	simplified
12.	5.35	$5\frac{35}{100}$	$5\frac{7}{20}$
13.	7.500	$7\frac{500}{1000}$	$7\frac{1}{2}$
14.	4.125	$4\frac{125}{1000}$	$4\frac{1}{8}$
15.	5.666	$5\frac{666}{1000}$	$5\frac{2}{3}$
16.	9.8	$9\frac{8}{10}$	$9\frac{4}{5}$

17. Jim needs $6\frac{1}{4}$ pounds of nails. $6.25 = 6\frac{25}{100} = 6\frac{1}{4}$

USE WHAT YOU HAVE LEARNED

Three digit decimal numbers represent thousandths.

	decimal	fraction	simplified			decimal	fraction	simplified
1.	.125	$\frac{125}{1000}$	$\frac{1}{8}$		2.	.875	$\frac{875}{1000}$	$\frac{7}{8}$
3.	.500	$\frac{500}{1000}$	$\frac{1}{2}$		4.	.250	$\frac{250}{1000}$	$\frac{1}{4}$

5. $\frac{2}{5}$ of the employees received raises. $.4 = \frac{4}{10} = \frac{2}{5}$

6. .08 is expressed as $\frac{2}{25}$. $.08 = \frac{8}{100} = \frac{2}{25}$

7. $\frac{12}{25}$ of the employees are women. $.48 = \frac{48}{100} = \frac{24}{50} = \frac{12}{25}$

8. $\frac{7}{8}$ of those surveyed rated the product A+. $.875 = \frac{875}{1000} = \frac{7}{8}$

9. Marie has filled $\frac{3}{4}$ of her quota. $.75 = \frac{75}{100} = \frac{3}{4}$

10. Ester earns $82. $10.25 = 10\frac{25}{100} = 10\frac{1}{4}$ $10\frac{1}{4} = \frac{41}{5} \times 8 = \frac{328}{4} = \$82$

LESSON 4 Metric Units   pages 11–14

EXERCISE 4A

1. $>$ (is greater than)

2. $>$ (is greater than)

3. $<$ (is less than)

4. $<$ (is less than)

5. Cord B is longer. Cord B is 18 meters $\times\ 3\frac{1}{4}$ feet $= \dfrac{18}{1} \times \dfrac{13}{1} = \dfrac{9}{1} \times \dfrac{13}{2} =$
$\dfrac{117}{2} = 58\frac{1}{2}$ feet

EXERCISE 4B

6. > (is greater than)

7. is the same as

8. is the same as

9. is the same as

10. Case B contains more oil.   One liter is larger than one quart.

EXERCISE 4C

11. > (is greater than)

12. is the same as

13. is the same as

14. is the same as

15. Supplier B is cheaper.   One kilogram is 2.2 times larger than one pound, so 100 kilograms is 2.2 times larger than 100 pounds.

USE WHAT YOU HAVE LEARNED

1. There are 1,000 millimeters in a meter.   10 millimeters per centimeter $\times$ 10 centimeters per decimeter $\times$ 10 decimeters per meter = 1,000 millimeters

2. There are 100 centiliters in a liter.   10 centiliters per deciliter $\times$ 10 decimeters per liter = 100 centiliters

3. There are 10,000 decigrams in a kilogram.   10 decigrams per gram $\times$ 1,000 grams per kilogram = 10,000 decigrams

4. John needs about 9 bags.
454 gm = 1 pound (given in chart)
454 divided by 50 = 9 R4, about 9 bags

5. If Mark buys one meter, he will have enough to make a pattern which calls for one yard.
1 meter (39 inches) is more than one yard (36 inches)
39 $\times$ 3 = 117   36 $\times$ 3 = 108
117 > 108

6. Aldo finds that he is serving 120 ml per glass.
1 ounce = 30 milliliters
30 $\times$ 4 = 120 milliliters

7. Roberto should load the truck waiting for 1,000 grams of fruit.
454 grams = 1 pound
1,000 grams (1 kilogram) = 2.2 pounds

8. Leon can move 10 bags of rice at a time.
454 gm = 1 pound
4540 gm = 10 pounds
10 bags × 10 pounds = 100 pounds

9. Each filter can process 10 million liters of water.
1 kiloliter = 1,000 liters
10,000 kiloliters × 1,000 = 10,000,000

LESSON 5 Rounding Decimals   pages 15–18

EXERCISE 5A

1. 1.6 $= (1.\cancel{6} + 1)$ $= 2$ **2.** 2.99 $= (2.\cancel{99} + 1)$ $= 3$

3. 6.2 $= 6.\cancel{2}$ $= 6$ **4.** 8.333 $= 8.\cancel{333}$ $= 8$

5. 5.50 $= (5.\cancel{50} + 1)$ $= 6$

Remember, when rounding to the nearest whole number, identify the number in the tenths place. If it is 4 or less, drop it and any other numbers to its right. If it is greater than 4, add 1 to the ones value and drop any numbers to the right of the decimal.

6. Jack counts 39 cords of wood. 10.5 is 11 rounded to the nearest whole number. 15.3 is 15 rounded to the nearest whole number. 12.9 is 13 rounded to the nearest whole number. 11 + 15 + 13 = 39

EXERCISE 5B

7. 1.563 $= (1.5\cancel{63} + .1)$ $= 1.6$ **8.** 2.590 $= (2.5\cancel{90} + .1)$ $= 2.6$

9. 6.22 $= 6.2\cancel{2}$ $= 6.2$ **10.** 8.435 $= 8.4\cancel{35}$ $= 8.4$

11. 5.55 $= (5.5\cancel{5} + .1)$ $= 5.6$

Remember, when rounding to the nearest tenth, identify the number in the hundredths place. If it is 4 or less, drop it and any other numbers to its right. If it is greater than 4, add 1 to the tenths value and drop any numbers to the right of the tenths place.

12. Mark has 2.4 lots of 1 inch pipe and 1.5 lots of 1.5 inch pipe. 2.36 is 2.4 rounded to the nearest tenth. 1.49 is 1.5 rounded to the nearest tenth.

EXERCISE 5C

13. 7.777 $= (7.77\cancel{7} + .01)$ $= 7.78$ **14.** 9.432 $= 9.43\cancel{2}$ $= 9.43$

15. 4.567 $= (4.56\cancel{7} + .01)$ $= 4.57$ **16.** 5.555 $= (5.55\cancel{5} + .01)$ $= 5.56$

17. 1.123 $= 1.12\cancel{3}$ $= 1.12$

Remember, when rounding to the nearest hundredth, identify the number in the thousandths place. If it is 4 or less, drop it and any other numbers to its right. If it is greater than 4, add 1 to the hundredths value and drop any numbers to the right of the hundredths place.

18.

Date	Order #	Computed Cost	Price
9/25/95	00123	14.255	$14.26
	00124	18.749	$18.75
	00125	39.3333	$39.33

Remember, when rounding to the nearest hundredth, identify the number in the thousandths place. If it is 4 or less, drop it and any other numbers to its right. If it is greater than 4, add 1 to the hundredths value and drop any numbers to the right of the hundredths place.

USE WHAT YOU HAVE LEARNED

1.

Decimal number	Round to hundredths	Round to tenths	Round to ones
10.549	10.55	10.5	11
25.089	25.09	25.1	25
1.493	1.49	1.5	1
9.769	9.77	9.8	10
33.333	33.33	33.3	33

2. Aikiko had 10.6 meters of blue silk, 5.8 meters of red silk, and 32 meters of yellow silk.
$10.55 = (10.55 + .1) = 10.6$
$5.79 = (5.79 + .1) = 5.8$
$32.00 = 32.00 = 32.0$

3. Allan drove 39.26 miles.
$39.255 = (39.255 + .01) = 39.26$

4. 34.667 dollars is $34.67.
34.667 dollars $= (34.667 + .01) = \$34.67$

5. Anna rounds up to $2,005.34.
$2,005.335$ dollars $= (2,005.335 + .01) = \$2,005.34$

6.

Date	Order #	Weight	Wt. rounded
9/25/95	00123	12.33 lb.	12.3 lb.
	00124	18.64 lb.	18.6 lb.
	00125	29.37 lb.	29.4 lb.

Remember, when rounding to the nearest tenth, identify the number in the hundredths place. If it is 4 or less, drop it and any other numbers to its right. If it is greater than 4, add 1 to the tenths value and drop any numbers to the right of the tenths place.

7. Bill has 5 full boxes, so he will have to buy 7 more.

53 divided by 10 = 5 boxes and $\frac{3}{10}$ or 5.3 boxes

5.3 rounded to nearest whole number is 5.0.
12 boxes less 5 boxes = 7 boxes must be purchased.
First convert discs to boxes, round to nearest whole number and then subtract from 12.

EXERCISE 6

	A	B	C
1.	1.5	<	2.5
2.	1.5̶5̶ = 1.6	=	1.6
3.	3.4̶9̶ = 3.5	>	3.4̶4̶ = 3.4
4.	7.8̶4̶ = 7.8	<	7.8̶5̶ = 7.9
5.	0.1̶9̶ = 0.20	=	0.2

6. 32.8 is greater than 32.75.   Adding a zero in the hundredths place of 32.8 gives you 32.80, which is clearly larger than 32.75.

USE WHAT YOU HAVE LEARNED

	A	B	C
1.	9.36̶4̶ = 9.36	<	9.36̶7̶ = 9.37
2.	5.25̶2̶ = 5.25	<	5.25̶5̶ = 5.26
3.	8.23̶4̶ = 8.23	<	8.23̶5̶ = 8.24
4.	1.11̶5̶ = 1.12	=	1.11̶9̶ = 1.12
5.	3.35̶3̶ = 3.35	=	3.35̶4̶ = 3.54

6. Bag #1, Bag #3, and Bag #4 need more nails.
   Bag #1 = 0.870   <   .995
   Bag #2 = 0.995   =   .995
   Bag #3 = 0.750   <   .995
   Bag #4 = 0.969   <   .995
   Bag #5 = 0.999   >   .995

7. All three lots are of a suitable size.
   Lot 25 1.555 acres = 1.6
   Lot 48 1.899 acres = 1.9
   Lot 65 1.479 acres = 1.5

8. Anna can make Pattern B.
   Pattern A 3.78 meters > 3.75
   Pattern B 3.72 meters < 3.75
   Pattern C 3.77 meters > 3.75

9. John can safely drive to Destination B.
   30 miles × 3 = 90 miles
   Destination A 90.5 miles > 90 miles
   Destination B 85.333 miles = 85 miles < 90 miles

10. 3.355 is the farthest distance.
    2.47 miles = 2.470
    3.352 miles = 3.352
    3.355 miles = 3.355

11. Packages A and B qualify for the cheaper rate.
Package A 2.444 lb. = 2.444 = 2.4
Package B 2.499 lb. = 2.499 = 2.5
Package C 2.555 lb. = 2.555 = 2.6

CHAPTER 1 Summary   pages 22–24

EXERCISE A

1. 701.407 and 9.409 have zero in the hundredths place.

2. 401.007 and 54.021 have zero in the tenths place.

If you have any trouble, refer to Lesson 1.

EXERCISE B

3. .034 is thirty-four thousandths

4. 42.28 is forty-two and twenty-eight hundredths

5. Three hundred twenty-six and three tenths is written 326.3

6. Two hundred and three hundredths is written 200.03

If you have any trouble, refer to Lesson 2.

EXERCISE C

7. $.67 = \dfrac{67}{100}$ $\dfrac{67}{100}$ is simplified to lowest terms

8. $.4 = \dfrac{2}{5}$ $\dfrac{4}{10}$ simplifies to $\dfrac{2}{5}$ **9.** $.425 = \dfrac{17}{40}$ $\dfrac{425}{1000}$ simplifies to $\dfrac{17}{40}$

If you have any trouble, refer to Lesson 3.

EXERCISE D

10. .76 = .8   **11.** .44 = .4   **12.** .426 = .4

13. .264 = .26   **14.** 0.694 = .69   **15.** .7618 = .76

If you have any trouble, refer to Lesson 5.

EXERCISE E

16. .16 > .1569   **17.** .6 > .4999   **18.** .3376 > .33

If you have any trouble, refer to Lesson 6.

CHAPTER 1 Math at Work   pages 25–28

1. Daphne will make $9.00.

$.75 = \dfrac{3}{4}$

$\$12 \times \dfrac{3}{4} = \$9$ inches

2. His odometer should read 0.5.

$$\frac{1}{2} = .5$$

3. The total of these three containers will fill half of her tank.

$$.5 = \frac{1}{2}$$

$$.25 = \frac{1}{4}$$

$$.25 = \frac{1}{4}$$

$$\frac{1}{2} + \frac{1}{4} + \frac{1}{4} =$$

$$\frac{1}{2} + \frac{2}{4} =$$

$$\frac{1}{2} + \frac{1}{2} = 1 \text{ gallon}$$

1 gallon divided by 2 gallons = .5

4. Barry has completed .7 of the trip.

$$\frac{210 \text{ miles}}{300 \text{ miles}} = \frac{7}{10} = 7$$

5. $\frac{4}{10}$ or .4 of Barry's tank is left.

1 gallon = 30 miles
full tank 10 gallons = 300 miles
180 miles divided by 30 miles = 6 gallons
300 − 180 = 120
120 divided by 30 miles = 4 gallons

$$\frac{4 \text{ gallons}}{10 \text{ gallons}} = \frac{4}{10} \text{ or } \frac{2}{5}$$

$$\frac{2}{5} = .4$$

6. .28 inch is the largest tube.
.280   largest
.255
.095   smallest

7. Yes, David has enough lattice. A meter is about 39 inches, and 50 cm is $\frac{1}{2}$ meter. David has a piece of fiberglass lattice that is about $19\frac{1}{2}$ inches wide and 78 inches long to cover an area that is 12 inches wide by 46 inches long.

8. 4 yards of netting is < 4 meters of netting.
1.1 yard = 1 meter
1 yard < 1 meter
4 yards < 4 meters

9. It will take 5 hours to administer 1 liter of solution.   1 liter is 100 centiliters, so 100 ÷ 20 = 5.

10. The contractions are 6 minutes apart. One hour is 60 minutes. One meter is 100 centimeters. 10 centimeters is $\frac{10}{100}$ or $\frac{1}{10}$ meter. $60 \times \frac{1}{10} = 6$ minutes.

11. The tank can hold the equivalent of 133 oil changes. The mixed decimal 3.75 can be converted to the mixed fraction $3\frac{75}{100}$: $3\frac{75}{100} = 3\frac{3}{10} = \frac{15}{4}$; $\frac{500}{1} \div \frac{15}{4} = \frac{500}{1} \times \frac{4}{15} = \frac{100}{1} \times \frac{4}{3} = \frac{400}{3} = \frac{133\ 1}{3} = 133$, to the nearest whole number.

12. Molly should enter $2,747.23.

13. $39.255 = 39.26$

14. 1,003.935 dollars = 1,003.935 = $1,003.94

15. Alex will need 9 meters of pipe.
    1.55 = 1.55 = 1.6 = 2
    2.66 = 2.66 = 2.7 = 3
    3.75 = 3.75 = 3.8 = 4
    2 + 3 + 4 = 9

16. Only one bag, Bag #1, must be removed.
    Bag #1 = 0.877 = 0.877 = 0.88
    Bag #2 = 0.945 = 0.945 = 0.95
    Bag #3 = 0.950 = 0.950 = 0.95
    Bag #4 = 0.949 = 0.949 = 0.95
    Bag #5 = 0.955 = 0.955 = 0.96

17. Lots 25 and 65 meet Joanne's specifications.
    Lot 25 1.455 = 1.46 = 1.5
    Lot 48 1.859 = 1.86 = 1.9
    Lot 65 1.479 = 1.48 = 1.5

18. Anna has enough material to make Pattern B.
    Pattern A $3\frac{3}{4}$ meters = 3.75 > 3.66
    Pattern B $3\frac{2}{3}$ meters = 3.66 = 3.66
    Pattern C 3.76 meters = 3.76 > 3.66

19. John can drive to Destination A safely.
    21 miles × 3 gallons = 63 miles
    Destination A 50.5 miles = 50.500 = 51 < 63 miles
    Destination B 65.333 miles = 65.333 = 65 > 63 miles

20. Package A qualifies for the less expensive rate.
    Package A 2.744 lb. = 2.74 < 2.75
    Package B 2.799 lb. = 2.78 > 2.75
    Package C 2.755 lb. = 2.76 > 2.75

21. The best price is c.
    a. two dollars and nine hundred fifty thousandths = $2.950
    b. two dollars and eighty-nine hundredths = $2.89
    c. two dollars and ninety-five thousandths = $2.095 = $2.10

22. Chris brought in $210.
.50 hr = $30
.35 hr = $30.
.75 hr = $30 + $20
.66 hr = $30 + $20
.87 hr = $30 + $20
$150 + $60 = $210

23. Friday, Pat produced the greatest amount, therefore he earned the most money.
Mon = .979 gross
Tue = .898 gross
Wed = .995 gross
Thu = .985 gross
Fri = .997 gross

24. Salesperson #2 had the highest total.
Salesperson #1 shipped a total of 495.335 lb.
Salesperson #2 shipped a total of 495.536 lb.
Salesperson #3 shipped a total of 495.455 lb.

LESSON 7 Adding Decimals

EXERCISE 7A

1. 2.4
    +5.3
    ———
    7.7

2. 18.7
    +11.9
    ————
    30.6

3. 42.5
    +28.6
    ————
    71.1

4. 23.9
    +10.4
    ————
    34.3

Write the decimal points in a straight column. Add the tenths column. If necessary, regroup the tenths and ones. Add the ones column. If necessary, regroup the tens and ones. Add the tens column.

5. 26.2 + 11.9 = 38.1   The question asks you to determine the sum of the miles on the highway (26.2) and the miles to the gate (11.9).

EXERCISE 7B

6. 5.22
    +1.74
    ————
    6.96

7. 33.08
    +18.73
    —————
    51.81

8. 56.49
    +30.96
    —————
    87.45

9. 295.35
    +162.28
    ——————
    457.63

Write the decimal points in a straight column. Add the hundredths column. If necessary, regroup the hundredths and tenths places. Add the tenths column. If necessary, regroup the tenths place and the ones place. Add the ones column. If necessary, regroup the ones place and the tens place. Add the tens column. If necessary, regroup the tens place and the hundreds place, and add the hundreds column.

10. $9.50 + $2.47 = $11.97   The question asks you to determine the sum of a bill that has a service charge ($9.50) and a sales tax ($2.47).

USE WHAT YOU HAVE LEARNED

1. 8.4
    +6.3
    ———
    14.7

2. 93.57
    +41.23
    —————
    134.80

3. 28.62
    19.08
    +15.75
    —————
    63.45

Write the decimal points in a straight column. If present, add the hundredths column. If necessary, regroup the hundredths and tenths places. Add the tenths column. If necessary, regroup the tenths place and the ones place. Add the ones column. If necessary, regroup the ones place and the tens place, and add the tens column.

4. 3.5 + 2.5 = 6.0   The question asks you to determine the sum of 3.5 and 2.5 gallons of gas.

5. 6.3 + 2.8 + 7.4 = 16.5   The question asks you to determine the sum of 6.3, 2.8 and 7.4 inches of rain.

6. 17.33 + 23.69 = 41.02   The question asks you to determine the sum of a fence that is 17.33 and 23.69 meters long.

7. .98 + .23 + .76 = 1.97   The question asks you to determine the sum of three pieces of gold that weigh .98, .23, and .76 ounces.

8. $8.3 + 2.7 = 11.0$ The question asks you to determine the sum of the width of a pool that is 8.3 meters wide with a 2.7 meters jacuzzi added.

9. $\$23.95 + \$47.86 = \$71.81$ The question asks you to determine the sum of business cards costing $23.95 and bills that cost $23.95.

LESSON 8 Adding Decimals with Different Place Values

pages 33–35

EXERCISE 8

1.	2.300	2.	6.0000	3.	.014	4.	.003
	26.000		.6000		7.600		.300
	$+$ .003		$+$ .0006		$+11.000$		$+237.000$
	28.303		6.6006		18.614		237.303

Align the decimal points in a column. Write zeros where necessary to give all of the values the same number of decimal places.

5. $9.8 = 2.4 + 3.0 + 4.4$ Mary travels 9.8 miles each day.

USE WHAT YOU HAVE LEARNED

1.	.300	2.	6.3	3.	.100	4.	.005
	2.600		19.0		9.452		.023
	$+$ .009		$+142.0$		$+2.000$		$+421.000$
	2.909		167.3		11.552		421.028
5.	16.000	6.	3.0000	7.	.023	8.	.034
	.010		5.0000		5.400		.600
	$+$ .003		$+$ .0006		$+21.000$		$+10.000$
	16.013		8.0006		26.423		10.634

Align the decimal points in a column. Write zeros where necessary to give all of the values the same number of decimal places.

9. $4.62 = 2.30 + 1.85 + .47$ The total time of the three reactions was 4.62 seconds.

10. $19.17 = 16.89 + 1.39 + .89$ Bill's total purchase was $19.17.

11. $20.42 = 11.22 + 6.00 + 3.20$ The total weight of plastic refuse collected for the week was 20.42 pounds.

12. $3.25 = 2.00 + 1.25$ The trip will take 3.25 hours.

13. $6.334 = 4.034 + .800 + 1.500$ The total weight of John's package is 6.334 ounces.

14. $38.48 = 14.28 + 11.20 + 13.00$ The total weight of the three fish is 38.48 pounds.

EXERCISE 9A

1. 9.3
   −6.4
   2.9

2. 38.1
   −22.5
   15.6

3. 70.6
   −49.7
   20.9

4. 531.9
   −286.4
   245.5

Regroup the tenths and ones if necessary. Subtract the tenths column. Regroup the ones and tens if necessary. Subtract the ones column. Regroup the tens and hundreds if necessary. Subtract the tens column. Subtract the hundreds column if necessary.

5. $9.8 − 1.2 = 8.6$ The question asks you to determine the difference between the present interest rate (9.8) and how much the rate will drop (1.2).

EXERCISE 9B

6. 2.62
   −1.95
   .67

7. 31.46
   −20.79
   10.67

8. 91.84
   −75.03
   16.81

9. 639.41
   −507.16
   132.25

Regroup the hundredths and tenths if necessary. Subtract the hundredths column. Regroup the tenths and ones if necessary. Subtract the tenths column. Regroup the ones and tens if necessary. Subtract the ones column. Regroup the tens and hundreds if necessary. Subtract the tens column if necessary. Subtract the hundreds column if necessary.

10. $364.52 − 108.73 = 255.79$ The question asks you to determine the difference between the number of acres a family owns (364.52) and the number of acres they want o keep when the rest of the land is sold (108.73).

USE WHAT YOU HAVE LEARNED

1. 27.3
   −18.1
   9.2

2. 49.62
   −25.95
   23.67

3. 59.004
   −16.293
   42.711

Regroup the thousandths and hundredths if necessary. Subtract the thousandths column if necessary. Regroup the hundredths and tenths if necessary. Subtract the hundredths column if necessary. Regroup the tenths and ones if necessary. Subtract the tenths column. Regroup the ones and tens if necessary. Subtract the ones column. Regroup the tens and hundreds if necessary. Subtract the tens column. Subtract the hundreds column if necessary.

4. $13.2 = 31.4 − 18.2$ The question asks you to determine the difference between the dumbbell weight (31.4) and the weight the client wants the dumbbells to be (18.2).

5. $\$24.75 = \$36.29 − \$11.54$ The question asks you to determine the difference between the total cost of office supplies ($36.29) and the cost of the supplies for the office ($24.75).

6. $18.80 = 47.38 − 28.58$ The question asks you to determine the difference between the total number of miles of the road (47.38) and the number of miles completed (28.58).

7. $154.89 = 321.93 - 167.04$ The question asks you to determine the difference between the weight of the recyclable (321.93) and the weight of the cans (167.04).

8. This is a multi-step problem. To find the overall width, add the width of the banner and the length of the ropes: $10.7 + 12.5 = 23.2$. To find how far off the ground the banner will be, subtract the height of the building from the combined length of the banner and ropes: $34.3 - 23.2 = 11.1$. The banner will hang 11.1 feet off the ground.

9. This is a multi-step problem. To find if both pieces can be cut from the board, subtract the length of the board from the first piece to be cut: $7.33 - 4.75 = 2.58$. The second board can be cut from what is left. To find how much more needs to be cut, subtract what is left from the second piece Martin needs: $2.58 - 2.55 = .03$. Martin will have to cut another .03 feet from the board.

LESSON 10 Subtracting Decimals with Different Place Values   pages 39–42

EXERCISE 10A

1. $\begin{array}{r} 7.0 \\ -2.3 \\ \hline 4.7 \end{array}$
2. $\begin{array}{r} 13.5 \\ -11.0 \\ \hline 2.5 \end{array}$
3. $\begin{array}{r} 86.0 \\ -47.9 \\ \hline 38.1 \end{array}$
4. $\begin{array}{r} 74.3 \\ -00.9 \\ \hline 73.4 \end{array}$

Align the decimal points. Write zeros where necessary to provide all the values with the same number of decimal places.

5. $18.0 - 15.4 = 2.6$ The question asks you to determine the difference between the number of miles to the house (18.0) and how far Sam has already driven (15.4).

EXERCISE 10B

6. $\begin{array}{r} 8.00 \\ -0.14 \\ \hline 7.86 \end{array}$
7. $\begin{array}{r} 54.80 \\ -15.03 \\ \hline 39.77 \end{array}$
8. $\begin{array}{r} 67.00 \\ -21.44 \\ \hline 45.56 \end{array}$
9. $\begin{array}{r} 50.47 \\ -03.90 \\ \hline 46.57 \end{array}$

Align the decimal points. Write zeros where necessary to provide all the values with the same number of decimal places.

10. $\$20.00 - \$11.78 = \$8.22$ The question asks you to determine the difference between an amount of money given (\$20.00) and the cost of a taxi ride (\$11.78).

USE WHAT YOU HAVE LEARNED

1. $\begin{array}{r} 12.0 \\ -04.9 \\ \hline 7.1 \end{array}$
2. $\begin{array}{r} 56.2 \\ -30.0 \\ \hline 26.2 \end{array}$
3. $\begin{array}{r} 80.31 \\ -77.40 \\ \hline 2.91 \end{array}$
4. $\begin{array}{r} 61.00 \\ -09.58 \\ \hline 51.42 \end{array}$

5. $\begin{array}{r} 32.60 \\ -15.08 \\ \hline 17.52 \end{array}$
6. $\begin{array}{r} 43.00 \\ -20.07 \\ \hline 22.93 \end{array}$
7. $\begin{array}{r} 6.000 \\ -2.148 \\ \hline 3.852 \end{array}$
8. $\begin{array}{r} 38.170 \\ -00.543 \\ \hline 37.627 \end{array}$

Align the decimal points. Write zeros where necessary to provide all the values with the same number of decimal places.

9. $60.45 - 9.8 = 50.65$ The question asks you to determine the difference between the length of the wall (60.45) and the distance allowed for the electrical outlet (9.8).

10. This is a multi-step problem. To find the total weight of the roast and the steaks, add 7.5 and 9 pounds: $7.5 + 9 = 16.5$. To find how much is left for hamburger, subtract the total sirloin tip weight (23.38) from the weight of both meats (16.5): $23.38 - 16.5 = 6.88$. Max wrote 6.88 pounds on the package of hamburger.

11. $\$145.92 - \$50.00 = \$95.92$ The question asks you to determine the difference between the total cost of the merchandise ($145.92) and the cash payment ($50.00).

12. This is a multi-step problem. The question asks you to determine the difference between the width of the door (23.25) and the 2-inch edges. To find the edge width, add $2 + 2 = 4$. Find the difference between the door width and the edges: $23.25 - 4.00 = 19.25$. Pete needs to order boards that are 19.25 inches wide.

13. This is a multi-step problem. To find how long the window will be from the floor, add the window height and the distance from the floor: $6.0 + 1.8 = 7.8$. To find how far from the ceiling the window will be, subtract the height of the window from the ceiling: $10.0 - 7.8 = 2.2$. The window will be 2.2 feet from the ceiling.

14. This is a multi-step problem. To find the total length of the picture frame, add each side: $24.80 + 24.80 + 19.06 + 19.06 = 87.72$. Tran can use one length of frame material. To find how much framing material will be left, find the difference between the length of the material and the amount of frame needed: $96.00 - 87.72 = 8.28$. There will be 8.28 inches of frame material left.

CHAPTER 2 Summary

EXERCISE A

1.	2.	3.	4.
$\begin{array}{r} .3 \\ +.4 \\ \hline .7 \end{array}$	$\begin{array}{r} .26 \\ +.33 \\ \hline .59 \end{array}$	$\begin{array}{r} .27 \\ +.67 \\ \hline .94 \end{array}$	$\begin{array}{r} .678 \\ +.224 \\ \hline .902 \end{array}$

5.	6.	7.	8.
$\begin{array}{r} .88 \\ +.77 \\ \hline 1.65 \end{array}$	$\begin{array}{r} .456 \\ +.789 \\ \hline 1.245 \end{array}$	$\begin{array}{r} 2.47 \\ +22.98 \\ \hline 25.45 \end{array}$	$\begin{array}{r} 4.893 \\ +56.870 \\ \hline 61.763 \end{array}$

9.	10.	11.	12.
$\begin{array}{r} 2.789 \\ +456.700 \\ \hline 459.489 \end{array}$	$\begin{array}{r} .360 \\ 27.000 \\ +\ 2.365 \\ \hline 29.725 \end{array}$	$\begin{array}{r} 738.100 \\ 478 \\ +\ \ 4.000 \\ \hline 742.578 \end{array}$	$\begin{array}{r} 765.098 \\ .300 \\ +354.000 \\ \hline 1,119.398 \end{array}$

If you have any trouble, refer to Lessons 7 and 8.

13.	.36 −.11 **.25**	**14.**	.439 −.328 **.111**	**15.**	.468 −.056 **.412**	**16.**	.723 −.488 **.235**
17.	7.873 − .972 **6.901**	**18.**	23.453 −19.476 **3.977**	**19.**	53.870 − 5.879 **47.991**	**20.**	27.980 − .997 **26.983**

If you have any trouble, refer to Lessons 9 and 10.

CHAPTER 2 Math at Work pages 45–48

1. Allen purchased 27.79 gallons of gasoline.

8.29
9.00
+10.50
27.79

2. Mary spent $10.66.

$2.99
$2.29
$2.69
+$2.69
$10.66

3. There are 72.43 miles to be completed.

126.00 miles
− 53.57 miles
72.43

4. Claire should charge this customer $1,374.99 on his credit card.

$1,599.99 sale price
−$ 225.00 in cash
$1,374.99 on his credit card

5. Ernie will need 46.4 feet of baseboard molding to complete the job.

10.6′   (There are two walls of each dimension given.)
10.6′
12.6′
+12.6′
46.4

6. Bob will work 5.33 hours today.

Trip #1	1hr 20 min. =	1.33
Trip #2	30 min. =	.50
Trip #3	2 hr. =	2.00
Installations	1 hr 30 min. =	+1.50
Total hours worked		5.33

7. The remaining newspaper weighs 537.9 lb.

21,432.8 lb. when he drives it back on the scale at the end of the day
−20,555.0 lb. empty
    877.8 lb. collected

  877.8 lb. collected total
−339.9 lb. aluminum
  537.9 newspapers for recycling

8. Her total order weighed 20.75 lb.

10.5 lb. brisket,	10.50
8 ounces = .5 or $\frac{1}{2}$ pound	6.00
$12 \times \frac{1}{2} = 6$ pounds of steak	+ 4.25
4.25 lb. of ground beef	20.75 lb.

9. Mrs. Smith ordered 5.40 lb. of candy.

$2\frac{1}{4} =$ 2.25

$1\frac{1}{2} =$ 1.50

$1.65 = +1.65$

      5.40

10. The total time of these three reactions is 24.41 seconds.

7.94 seconds =   7.940
8.455 seconds =   8.455
8.01 seconds = +8.010
        24.405

24.405 = 24.41 seconds

11. They will have 19.85 ft. on the ropes to tie streamers.

  32.60 ft.
−12.75 ft.
  19.85 ft.

12. Iris should give him $46.31.

  $200.00
−$153.69
   $46.31

13. 12 ft −10.5 = 1.5 feet will be cut off each plank

20 × 1.5 = 30 feet total will be cut off

14.   6.75
     6.75
     4.75
+ 4.75
   23.00 ft. of molding to dress one window

23 × 4 = 92 ft. to dress all four windows

15. Starting balance = $25.14
                             −$ 1.49
                             $23.65
                             −$ 2.55
                             $21.10
                             −$ 9.89
     $11.21 Balance at the end of the month

16.   10.44 lb. salmon
            6.54 lb. catfish
         + 3.89 lb. shrimp
         20.87 lb. total weight

17. Starting balance = $1,023.56
                             $ 50.00
                           +$ 450.00
                             $1,523.56
                           −$ 68.79
                             $1,454.77
                           −$ 15.99
                             $1,438.78
                           −$ 9.00
     $1,429.78 Balance at the end of the month

18. $100.00 in Sam's expense account

     $100.00
     −$21.89
     $78.11
     −$15.77
     $62.34
     −$25.50
     $36.84 Balance in Sam's expense account

19.   .557 gm
           .749 gm
         +1.250 gm
         2.556 gm is the total weight in grams

20. 8.25 = .8.25
        9.   = 9.00
        8.5 = 8.50
        9.0 = 9.00
        8.25 = +8.25
         43.00 Jesus's total hours for the week

21. $ .43 $3.95
          $2.35 $ .89
          $1.85   +$1.23
          $1.95 $6.07 Weekly expenses
        +$2.10
          $8.68 Weekly income

          $8.68
        −$6.07
          $2.61 More than expenses

22. The carelessness of the workers cost his company $37.82.

$16.89
$12.95
$ 3.99
+$ 3.99
$37.82

23.   1.42
1.55
2.00
+2.25
7.22 Hours

24.   15.290 lb.
2.333 lb.
+ 5.500 lb.
23.123 lb. Total weight

CHAPTER 3 Multiplication with Decimals

LESSON 11 Multiplying Decimals   pages 49–51

EXERCISE 11

1. $10.00
    × 4
    ―――――
    $40.00

2. 7.889
    × 8
    ―――――
    63.112

3. 43.093
    × 55
    ―――――
    215465
    +2154650
    ―――――――
    2370.115

4. 93.035
    × 28
    ―――――
    744280
    +1860700
    ―――――――
    2604.980

Multiply. Place the decimal point after you finish multiplying. Count the total number of places to the right of the decimal point in the numbers being multiplied. Place the decimal point that number of spaces from the right in the answer.

5. Bill will earn a minimum of 1,332.80 per month. $333.2 \times 4 = 1332.80$

USE WHAT YOU HAVE LEARNED

1. 6.5
    × 7
    ―――――
    45.5

2. 9.09
    × 12
    ―――――
    1818
    +9090
    ―――――
    109.08

3. 21.93
    × 34
    ―――――
    8772
    +65790
    ―――――
    745.62

4. 439.088
    × 58
    ―――――
    3512704
    +21954400
    ―――――――
    25,467.104

5. 45.7904
    × 72
    ―――――
    915808
    +32053280
    ―――――――
    3,296.9088

6. 399.032
    × 2.46
    ―――――
    2394192
    15961280
    +79806400
    ―――――――
    981.61872

7. 87.4235
    × 4.9
    ―――――
    7868115
    +34969400
    ―――――――
    428.37515

8. 666.094
    × .3902
    ―――――
    1332188
    0000000
    599484600
    +1998282000
    ―――――――――
    259.9098788

Multiply. Place the decimal point after you finish multiplying. Count the total number of places to the right of the decimal point in the numbers being multiplied. Place the decimal point that number of spaces from the right in the answer.

9. Bill makes $17,326.40 per year. 333.20×52 weeks (in a year) = 17,326.40

10. Pierre's total payment is $6,504.84. 180.69×36 months = 6504.84

11. The recycling center will pay $25.09 (to the nearest cent).
    $.124 \times 202.3$ pounds = 25.0852

12. It costs $34.08 (to the nearest cent) for 121.7 miles.
    $.28 \times 121.7$ miles = 34.076

13. The nurse earns $450 for a 40 hour week. $11.25 \times 40 = 450$

14. She earned $238.50 in overtime. $15.90 \times 15 = 238.50$

15. The nurse's total pay was $688.50. $450 + 238.50 = 688.50$

LESSON 12 Multiplication by 10, 100, 1,000 pages 52–54

EXERCISE 12

1. $5.25	2. $14.55	3. .33	4. 7.089
$\times$ 10	$\times$ 100	$\times$ 1000	$\times$ 10
$52.50	$1,455	330	70.89

Remember, to multiply by 10, 100, or 1,000, move the decimal point in the product one place to the right for every zero in the multiplier.

5. 1000 copies would cost $35.00. $.035 \times 1000 = 35$

USE WHAT YOU HAVE LEARNED

1. $3.9 \times 10 = 39$

2. $6.7 \times 10 = 67$

3. $5.9 \times 100 = 590$

4. $9.5 \times 100 = 950$

5. $69.3 \times 10 = 693$

6. $5.8 \times 100 = 580$

7. $4.19 \times 100 = 419$

8. $7.27 \times 1,000 = 7,270$

9. $70.35 \times 100 = 7,035$

10. $67.02 \times 100 = 6,702$

11. $30.09 \times 1000 = 30,090$

12. $6694.1 \times 1000 = 6,694,100$

13. $6.75 \times 100 = 675

14. $3.45 \times 10 = 34.5$

15. $90.60 \times 1000 = 90,600$

16. $.87 \times 100 = 87$

17. $3.89 \times 1000 = 3,890$

18. $55.89 \times 10 = 558.9$

19. $4.85 \times 1000 = $4,850$

20. $10.75 \times 10 = 107.5

Remember, to multiply by 10, 100, or 1,000, move the decimal point in the product one place to the right for every zero in the multiplier.

21. Edward pumps 80 gallons each day. $8 \times 10 = 80$.
Edward pumps 400 gallons each 5-day week. $80 \times 5 = 400$
Edward pumps 800 gallons in 10 days. $80 \times 10 = 800$
Edward's supervisor buys $903.20 of gas every 2 weeks.
$1.129 \times 800 = 903.2$

22. Pencils cost $4.00 per box. $.04 \times 100 = 4$

23. Pencils cost $30.00 for 1000. $.03 \times 1000 = 30$

24. 10 copies cost $ .43. $.043 \times 10 = .43$
100 copies cost $4.30. $.043 \times 100 = 4.3$
1000 copies cost $43.00. $.043 \times 1000 = 43$

25. Mark can save $7.40. $.074 \times 100 = 7.4$

EXERCISE 13

1. $7.25 × .1 = $ .725, or $ .73, rounded to the nearest cent.

2. $10.88 × .01 = $ .1088, or $ .11 rounded to the nearest cent.

3. 3.44 × .001 = .00344

   Remember, to multiply by .1, .01, or .001, move the decimal point one place to the left for every decimal place in the multiplier.

4. One can weighs 4.5 pounds × .01 cans = .045 pound per can.

USE WHAT YOU HAVE LEARNED

1. 2.3 × .01= .023

2. .46 × 0.01 = .0046

3. 260 × .001 = .26

4. .003 × .01= .00003

   Remember, to multiply by .1, .01, or .001, move the decimal point one place to the left for every decimal place in the multiplier.

5. The electric motor costs $ .0035 to operate for .1 hour.   .035 × .1 = .0035

6. It takes .355 gallon of fertilizer for one tenth of an acre.   3.55 × . 1 = .355

7. Each copy costs $ .053.   53 × .001 = .053

8. .0003 gram was all that was allowed.   .03 × .01 = .0003

9. Brian has 30 seconds before he misses his exit.   60 seconds × .5 = 30 seconds. 60 miles per hour is one mile per minute (an hour is 60 minutes, and 60 miles ÷ 60 minutes = 1 mile per minute). There are 60 seconds in a minute.

10. Dora can expect $28.00.   28,000 × .001 = 28

LESSON 14 Working with the Metric System   pages 57-59

EXERCISE 14

1. The metric unit that measures weight is the gram.

2. The metric unit that measures length is the meter.

3. The metric unit that measures volume is the liter.

4. hecto means 100 ×

5. centi means .01 ×

6. deca (deka) means 10 ×

7. deci means .1 ×

8. kilo means 1000 ×

9. milli means .001 ×

10. 4 kilometers = 4,000 meters

11. 5 centimeters = .05 meters

12. 5 decaliters = 50 liters

13. 2 deciliters = .2 liter

6. $4.2 \times 10^5 = 4.2 \times 10 \times 10 \times 10 \times 10 \times 10 = 420,000$
7. $4.34 \times 10^7 = 4.34 \times 10 \times 10 \times 10 \times 10 \times 10 \times 10 \times 10 = 43,400,000$
8. $.15 \times 10^6 = .15 \times 10 \times 10 \times 10 \times 10 \times 10 \times 10 = 150,000$
9. $78.3 \times 10^5 = 78.3 \times 10 \times 10 \times 10 \times 10 \times 10 = 7,830,000$
10. 3,744,000 vehicles go through the intersection each year.
    $3.744 \times 10 \times 10 \times 10 \times 10 \times 10 \times 10 = 3,744,000$

USE WHAT YOU HAVE LEARNED

1. $5^2 = 5 \times 5 = 25$
2. $4^3 = 4 \times 4 \times 4 = 64$
3. $9^4 = 9 \times 9 \times 9 \times 9 = 6,561$
4. $6^5 = 6 \times 6 \times 6 \times 6 \times 6 = 7,776$
5. $4.3 \times 10^5 = 4.3 \times 10 \times 10 \times 10 \times 10 \times 10 = 430,000$
6. $6 \times 10^6 = 6 \times 10 \times 10 \times 10 \times 10 \times 10 \times 10 = 6,000,000$
7. $7.004 \times 10^7 = 7.004 \times 10 \times 10 \times 10 \times 10 \times 10 \times 10 \times 10 = 70,040,000$
8. $3.12 \times 10^8 = 3.12 \times 10 \times 10 \times 10 \times 10 \times 10 \times 10 \times 10 \times 10 = 312,000,000$

9. Shipping used 43,000 feet of strapping tape.
   $4.3 \times 10 \times 10 \times 10 \times 10 = 43,000.$

10. Each side will be 2 feet long.

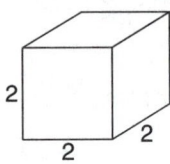

11. 2,234,000. $2.234 \times 10 \times 10 \times 10 \times 10 \times 10 \times 10 = 2,234,000$

12. 46,656 cubic inches. $36 \times 36 \times 36 = 46,656$

13. There are 3,900,000 radios in the city.
    $3.9 \times 10 \times 10 \times 10 \times 10 \times 10 \times 10 = 3,900,000$

14. It is a 220,000 ohm resistor. $2.2 \times 10 \times 10 \times 10 \times 10 \times 10 = 220,000$

CHAPTER 3 Summary   pagea 64–66

1.
$$\begin{array}{r} \$20.00 \\ \times \quad 3 \\ \hline \$60.00 \end{array}$$

2.
$$\begin{array}{r} 6.778 \\ \times \quad 7 \\ \hline 47.446 \end{array}$$

3.
$$\begin{array}{r} 52.104 \\ \times \quad 66 \\ \hline 312624 \\ +3126240 \\ \hline 3,438.864 \end{array}$$

4.
$$\begin{array}{r} 82.024 \\ \times \quad 17 \\ \hline 574168 \\ +820240 \\ \hline 1,394.408 \end{array}$$

5.
$$
\begin{array}{r}
8.5 \\
\times\ \ 8 \\
\hline
68.0
\end{array}
$$

6.
$$
\begin{array}{r}
6.06 \\
\times\ \ 14 \\
\hline
2424 \\
+6060 \\
\hline
84.84
\end{array}
$$

7.
$$
\begin{array}{r}
13.43 \\
\times\ \ 41 \\
\hline
1343 \\
+53720 \\
\hline
550.63
\end{array}
$$

8.
$$
\begin{array}{r}
4.098 \\
\times\ \ 52 \\
\hline
8196 \\
+204900 \\
\hline
213.096
\end{array}
$$

9.
$$
\begin{array}{r}
19.45 \\
\times\ \ .23 \\
\hline
5835 \\
+38900 \\
\hline
4.4735
\end{array}
$$

10.
$$
\begin{array}{r}
421.89 \\
\times\ \ 2.61 \\
\hline
2531340 \\
+8437800 \\
\hline
1{,}101.1329
\end{array}
$$

11.
$$
\begin{array}{r}
99.422 \\
\times\ \ .49 \\
\hline
894798 \\
+3976880 \\
\hline
48.71678
\end{array}
$$

12.
$$
\begin{array}{r}
611.09 \\
\times\ \ 3.4 \\
\hline
244436 \\
+1833270 \\
\hline
2{,}077.706
\end{array}
$$

If you have trouble, refer to Lesson 11.

EXERCISE B

13.
$$
\begin{array}{r}
69.3 \\
\times\ \ 10 \\
\hline
693.0
\end{array}
$$

14.
$$
\begin{array}{r}
5.8 \\
\times\ \ 100 \\
\hline
580.0
\end{array}
$$

15.
$$
\begin{array}{r}
4.19 \\
\times\ \ 100 \\
\hline
419.00
\end{array}
$$

16.
$$
\begin{array}{r}
7.27 \\
\times\ \ 1000 \\
\hline
7{,}270.00
\end{array}
$$

If you have trouble, refer to Lesson 12.

EXERCISE C

17.
$$
\begin{array}{r}
58.4 \\
\times\ \ .1 \\
\hline
5.84
\end{array}
$$

18.
$$
\begin{array}{r}
6.9 \\
\times .01 \\
\hline
.069
\end{array}
$$

19.
$$
\begin{array}{r}
2.21 \\
\times\ \ .01 \\
\hline
.0221
\end{array}
$$

20.
$$
\begin{array}{r}
8.37 \\
\times .001 \\
\hline
.00837
\end{array}
$$

If you have trouble, refer to Lesson 13.

EXERCISE D

21. 2 kilometer = 2,000 meters   1 kilometer = 1,000 meters. 2 × 1,000 = 2,000

22. 4 centigrams = .4 decigrams   There are 10 centigrams in a decigram.

23. 6 hectoliters = 60,000 centiliters   There are 100 centiliters in a liter and 100 liters in a hectoliter. 100 × 100 = 10,000 centiliters in a hectoliter. 10,000 × 6 = 60,000.

24. 3 decameters = 300 decimeters   There are 10 decimeters in a meter and 10 meters in a decameter. 10 × 10 = 100 decimeters in a decameter. 100 × 3 = 300.

If you have trouble, refer to Lesson 14.

EXERCISE E

25. $2.4 \times 10^6 = 2.4 \times 10 \times 10 \times 10 \times 10 \times 10 \times 10 = 2{,}400{,}000$

26. $6.22 \times 10^5 = 6.22 \times 10 \times 10 \times 10 \times 10 \times 10 = 622{,}000$

27. $.26 \times 10^7 = .26 \times 10 \times 10 \times 10 \times 10 \times 10 \times 10 \times 10 = 2{,}600{,}000$

28. $14.3 \times 10^6 = 14.3 \times 10 \times 10 \times 10 \times 10 \times 10 \times 10 = 14{,}300{,}000$

If you have trouble, refer to Lesson 15.

1. The copy will be 6.375 inches by 8.25 inches.
    $8.5 \times .75 = 6.375$ $11 \times .75 = 8.25$ inches

2. The area of the patio is 120.785 square feet. $8.33 \times 14.5 = 120.785$

3. The area of the concrete walk is 57.75 square feet. $3.5 \times 16.5 = 57.75$

4. The distance is 3.5 miles. $1 \div 2 = \frac{1}{2}$ $\frac{1}{2} = .5$ $.5 \times 7 = 3.5$

5. The third package is 1.32 pounds. $3.5 - .88 - 1.3 = 1.32$

6. The pastrami costs $9.77. $2.79 \times 3.5 = 9.765$ *or* 9.77 to the nearest hundred

7. Julian earns $12.60 per hour when he works overtime. $8.40 \times 1.5 = 12.60$

8. Julian earned $411.60. $40 \times 8.40 = 336$ $6 \times 12.60 = 75.60$
    $336 + 75.60 = 411.60$

9. The copy is 10.125 centimeters wide by 11.25 centimeters long.
    $6.75 \times 1.5 = 10.125$ $7.5 \times 1.5 = 11.25$

10. The area is approximately 114 square centimeters.
    $10.125 \times 11.25 = 113.90625$, or 114 square centimeters, rounded off to the
    nearest whole centimeter

11. Doris should charge 46¢ for the plastic. $114 \times .004 = .456$, of 46 rounded to
    the nearest hundredth

12. The area of the flower beds is 193.5 square feet.
    $5.25 \times 6 = 31.5$ $4.5 \times 18 \times 2 = 162$ $31.5 + 162 = 193.5$

13. The area of the flower beds for 8 duplexes is 1,548 square feet.
    $193.5 \times 8 = 1,548$

14. John's bid would be $20,700. $1,548 \times 13.36 = 20,681.28$, or 20,700 to the
    nearest hundred

15. Taylor delivered 7,280 pounds of sand. $3.64 \times 2,000 = 7,280$

16. Valerie spent $56.22. $12.5 \times .48 = 6$ $46.5 \times 1.08 = 50.22$
    $6 + 50.22 = 56.22$

17. Mark has 68 cups of syrup. $4.5 \times 16 = 68$

18. The second copy will be .25 of the size of the original. $.5 \times .5 = .25$

19. Paul spent $97.09 on paint. $13.87 \times 7 = 97.09$

20. Paul can save $8.72 on paint. $13.87 \times 10 = 138.70$ $138.70 - 129.98 = 8.72$

21. 1.728×10^6 is 1,728,000. $1.728 \times 10 \times 10 \times 10 \times 10 \times 10 \times 10 = 1,728,000$

22. Meredith will spend $32.00 on stamps. $.32 \times 100 = 32$

23. John has to cover 6,852.125 square feet with sod. $80 \times 100 = 8,000$
    $14.75 \times 22.5 = 331.875$ $34 \times 12 \times 2 = 816$
    $8,000 - 331.875 - 816 = 6,852.125$

24. John will spend $1,817 on sod. $6,900 \div 3 = 2,300$ $2,300 \times .79 = 1,817$

LESSON 16 Dividing Decimals   **pages 71–75**

EXERCISE 16A

```
        3.2              7.75             4.08            27.312
1. 7)22.4        2. 6)46.50       3. 8)32.64       4. 15)409.680
    -21              -42              -32               -30
     14               45               06               109
    -14              -42              - 0              -105
      0               30               64                46
                     -30              -64               -45
                       0                0                18
                                                        -15
                                                         30
                                                        -30
                                                          0
```

Set the decimal point in the quotient directly above the decimal point in the dividend. If the division results in a remainder, add a zero to the dividend. Set this zero next to the remainder and divide again.

5. $1.8 = 21.6 \div 12$ The question asks you to determine the quotient when a 21.6 pound box of clay is divided between 12 students.

EXERCISE 16B

```
       16.6               .7              26.5             15.8
6. 5)83.0         7. 50)35.0       8. 12)318.0      9. 45)711.0
    -5                -350             -24              -45
    33                   0              78              261
   -30                                 -72             -225
    30                                  60              360
   -30                                 -60             -360
     0                                   0                0
```

Set a decimal point in the dividend after the ones place. Set a 0 in the tenths place. Set the decimal point in the quotient directly above the decimal point in the dividend. Divide.

10. $13.5 = 81 \div 6$ The question asks you to determine the quotient when a cabinet that is 81 inches tall is divided evenly to allow for 6 shelves.

USE WHAT YOU HAVE LEARNED

```
        4.8             26.05            25.94             8.75
1. 9)43.2        2. 11)286.55     3. 15)389.10     4. 8)70.00
    -36              -22              -30              -64
     72               66               89               60
    -72              -66              -75              -56
      0               05              141               40
                     - 0             -135              -40
                       55               60                0
                      -55              -60
                        0                0
```

If the dividend does not have a decimal point, set one to the right of the ones place. Set a zero in the tenths place. Set the decimal point in the quotient directly above the decimal point in the dividend. If the division results in a remainder, add a zero to the dividend. Set this zero next to the remainder and divide again.

5. $54.8 \div 2 = 27.4$ The question asks you to determine the quotient when a hedge that is 54.8 feet long has a plant every 2 feet.

6. $64 \div 10 = 6.4$ The question asks you to determine whether to use a 6, 8, or 12-ounce cup to hold juice. Divide the number of ounces of juice (64) by the number of children (10). Each child will get 6.4 ounces of juice. The 8-ounce cup will be used. The 6 ounce is too small and the 12-ounce cup is too big.

7. $28 \div 40 = .7$ The question asks you to determine the quotient when 28 acres of land is divided into 40 lots.

8. This problem is a multi-step problem. To find how much money will be divided between the four workers, subtract the amount of money to go toward supplies ($75) from the total money earned ($665): $665 − $75 = $590. To find how much money each worker will earn, divide the amount left ($590) by the number of workers (4): $590 ÷ 4 = $147.50. Each worker will get $147.50.

9. This problem is a multi-step problem. To find how much wall space is left once the sofa is in place, subtract the sofa length (74 inches) from the length of the wall (171 inches): $171 − 74 = 97$. To find how many inches will be on each side of the sofa, divide the wall space left (97 inches) by 2: $97 \div 2 = 48.5$. The sofa will be placed 48.5 inches from the end of the wall.

10. This problem is a multi-step problem. To find how much each drink costs Jane, divide the case price ($3.60) by the number of drinks in a case (24): $3.60 \div 24 = \$.15$ or 15¢. To find how much Jane will charge for each drink, add the cost of each drink (15¢) and the profit she wants to get (30¢): $15¢ + 30¢ = 45¢$. Jane will charge 45¢ for each drink.

LESSON 17 Decimal Remainders   pages 76–80

EXERCISE 17A

1.
$$
\begin{array}{r}
3.133 \\
6)\overline{18.800} \\
-18 \\
\hline
08 \\
-\ 6 \\
\hline
20 \\
-18 \\
\hline
20 \\
-18 \\
\hline
2
\end{array}
$$

2.
$$
\begin{array}{r}
4.55 \\
9)\overline{41.00} \\
-36 \\
\hline
50 \\
-45 \\
\hline
50 \\
-45 \\
\hline
5
\end{array}
$$

3.
$$
\begin{array}{r}
3.522 \\
27)\overline{95.100} \\
-81 \\
\hline
141 \\
-135 \\
\hline
60 \\
-54 \\
\hline
60 \\
-54 \\
\hline
6
\end{array}
$$

4.
$$
\begin{array}{r}
50.77 \\
18)\overline{914.00} \\
-90 \\
\hline
14 \\
-\ 0 \\
\hline
140 \\
-126 \\
\hline
14
\end{array}
$$

When you find that the remainder is repeating itself, stop dividing and place a bar above the repeating numbers in the quotient.

5. $28 \div 12 = 2.33$ The question asks you to determine the quotient when 28 yards of materials is divided into 12 cushions.

6. 6.09
```
      6.085
  7)42.600
   −42
     06
   −  0
     60
    −56
     40
    −35
      5
```

7. 2.43
```
      2.427
 22)53.400
   −44
     94
    −88
     60
    −44
    160
   −154
      6
```

8. 5.36
```
      5.357
 14)75.000
   −70
     50
    −42
     80
    −70
    100
   − 98
      2
```

9. 15.72
```
     15.724
 37)581.800
   −37
    211
   −185
    268
   −259
     90
    −74
    160
   −148
     12
```

If the number in the thousandths place is greater than 4, then add 1 to the number in the hundredth place. If the number in the thousandths place is 4 or less, then the number in the hundredths place remains unchanged. In either case, omit the number from the thousandths place.

10. $65 \div 32 = 2.03$, to the nearest hundredth   The question asks you to determine the quotient when 65 pounds of candy is divided equally into 32 boxes.

USE WHAT YOU HAVE LEARNED

1. 3.51
```
      3.514
  7)24.600
   −21
     36
    −35
     10
   −  7
     30
    −28
      2
```

2. 8.33
```
      8.333
  9)75.000
   −72
     30
    −27
     30
    −27
     30
    −27
      3
```

3. 12.15

$$\begin{array}{r} 12.148 \\ 27\overline{)328.000} \\ -27 \\ \hline 58 \\ -54 \\ \hline 40 \\ -27 \\ \hline 130 \\ -108 \\ \hline 220 \end{array}$$

4. 10.46

$$\begin{array}{r} 10.462 \\ 16\overline{)167.400} \\ -16 \\ \hline 074 \\ -64 \\ \hline 100 \\ -96 \\ \hline 40 \\ -32 \\ \hline 8 \end{array}$$

If the number in the thousandths place is greater than 4, then add 1 to the number in the hundredth place. If the number in the thousandths place is 4 or less, then the number in the hundredths place remains unchanged. In either case, omit the number from the thousandths place.

5. $1{,}235 \div 3 = 411.\overline{66}$ or 411.7 miles   The question asks you to determine the quotient when 1,235 miles is divided by 3 days.

6. $139 \div 8 = 17.375$ or 18 pipes   The question asks you to divide 139 feet by 8 feet. Neil needs exactly 17.375 pipes. That is 17 full pipes and 1 3-foot piece. Rounded to the nearest whole pipe, Neil needs 17 pipes. Assuming he has to buy full lengths of pipe, he will have to buy 18 pipes, with 5 feet left over. If you rounded to the nearest whole number, your answer was 17.

7. $\$13.48 \div 35 = \$.385\overline{142857}$ or $\$.39$ The question asks you to divide $13.48 by 35. Rounded to the nearest hundredth, the answer is 39¢ per questionnaire.

8. This problem is a multi-step problem. To find how far apart the lights will be, divide: $135 \div 13 = 10.384615$ feet or 10 feet, to the nearest whole foot. That means that, overall lights will be spaced over an area that is $13 \times 10 = 130$ feet long. The hall is 135 feet. This means that the hall is $135 - 130 = 5$ feet longer than distance between the two end lights. In order to center the lights, Jose needs to divide these remaining five feet evenly between the two ends: $5 \div 2 = 2.5.$ The end lights will fall 2.5 feet from the ends of the hallway.

9. Judy can put 1.833 batches of punch into the bowl. One batch of punch is 3 gallons: 1.2 (gallons of carbonated drink) + .8 (gallons of orange juice) + 1 (gallon of lemonade) = 3 gallons. Divide the capacity of the bowl by the size of the batch: $5.5 \div 3 = 1.833$ batches. Rounded to the nearest tenth, this is 1.8 batches. Judy can get just less than 2 full batches into the punch bowl.

10. Each bottle costs $3.33 on sale, rounded to the nearest hundredth: $\$39.99 \div 12 = \$3.3325.$ Each bottle costs $4.83 at the regular price, rounded to the nearest hundredth: $\$57.99 \div 12 = \$4.8325.$ People will save $1.50 per bottle: $\$4.83 - \$3.33 = \$1.50.$

1.
```
      30.18
   3)90.54
    −9
     005
    − 3
      24
     −24
       0
```

2.
```
      39.02
   4)156.08
    −12
      36
     −36
      008
     − 8
        0
```

3.
```
      60.03
  12)720.36
    −72
     0036
    − 36
        0
```

4. 307.17, to the nearest hundredth
```
       307.170
  15)4,607.560
   −4 5
     107
    −105
      25
     −15
      106
     −105
       10
```

If no complete groups of the divisor are present when you divide, then place the zero in the quotient and set the next value in the dividend beside the remainder. Divide again.

5. 1,806.3 ÷ 9 = 200.7   The question asks you to determine the quotient when 1,806.3 cubic yards of concrete is delivered in 9 cubic-yard trucks.

6. 16.00, to the nearest hundredth
```
     16.004
  5)80.020
   −5
    30
   −30
    0020
   − 20
      0
```

7. 30.01, to the nearest hundredth
```
     30.005
  2)60.010
   −6
    00010
   −   10
        0
```

8.

$$
\begin{array}{r}
20.01 \\
10\overline{)200.10} \\
\underline{-20} \\
0010 \\
\underline{-10} \\
0
\end{array}
$$

9. 500.18, to the nearest hundredth

$$
\begin{array}{r}
500.175 \\
14\overline{)7{,}002.450} \\
\underline{-70} \\
0024 \\
\underline{-\ 14} \\
105 \\
\underline{-\ 98} \\
70 \\
\underline{-70} \\
0
\end{array}
$$

If no complete groups of the divisor are present when you divide, then place the zero in the quotient and set the next value in the dividend beside the remainder. Divide again.

10. 1,206.09 ÷ 12 = 100.51, rounded to the nearest hundredth   The question asks you to determine the quotient when $1,206.09 worth of furniture is divided into 12 payments.

USE WHAT YOU HAVE LEARNED

1.

$$
\begin{array}{r}
10.05 \\
8\overline{)80.40} \\
\underline{-8} \\
0040 \\
\underline{-\ 40} \\
0
\end{array}
$$

2.

$$
\begin{array}{r}
500.9 \\
6\overline{)3{,}005.4} \\
\underline{-30} \\
0054 \\
\underline{-\ 54} \\
0
\end{array}
$$

3. 60.00, to the nearest hundreth

$$
\begin{array}{r}
60.00\overline{3} \\
15\overline{)900.050} \\
\underline{-90} \\
00050 \\
\underline{-\ 45} \\
5
\end{array}
$$

4. 30,000.14, to the nearest hundredth

$$
\begin{array}{r}
30000.141 \\
20\overline{)600002.830} \\
\underline{-60} \\
000028 \\
\underline{-\ 20} \\
83 \\
\underline{-80} \\
30 \\
\underline{-20} \\
10
\end{array}
$$

If no complete groups of the divisor are present when you divide, then place the zero in the quotient and set the next value in the dividend beside the remainder. Divide again.

5. 200.76 ÷ 4 = 50.19   The question asks you to determine the quotient when 200.76 quarts of juice is divided into gallons.

6. 2,008.0 ÷ 10 = 200.8   The question asks you to determine the quotient when 2,008 pounds of shrimp is divided equally between 10 stores.

7. The question asks you to determine the quotient for two problems. To find how much money Charla makes in a 9 hour day, divide the amount she earns daily ($350.00) by the number of hours she works (9): $350.00 ÷ 9 = $38.888 or $38.89. To find how much money Charla earns in a 5 hour day, divide the amount she earns ($350.00) by the number of hours she works (5): $350.00 ÷ 5 = $70.00.

8. This problem is a multi-step problem. To find how much time Mona has, multiply the number of hours (8) by the number of minutes in an hour (60): 8 × 60 = 480. Then divide the number of minutes (480) by the number of stops (6): 480 ÷ 6 = 80. To find the number of hours, take the number of minutes (80) and divide it by the number of minutes in an hour (60): 80 ÷ 60 = 1.33. Mona can spend 1.33 hours at each stop.

9. $100.95 ÷ 10 = $10.95   The question asks you to determine the quotient when $100.95 is divided by 10 customers.

10. This problem is a multi-step problem. To find the total cost of the car, add the cost of the car ($12,025.45) to the cost of fees and maintenance ($475.00): $12,025.45 + $475.00 = $12,500.45. To find how many times Joel must rent out the car before turning a profit, divide the total cost of the car ($12,500.00) by the amount he will rent it for ($125) : $12,500.45 ÷ $125 = 100.003. Joel will have to rent the car 100 times before he will make a profit on the car.

LESSON 19 Dividing by Decimals   pages 85–88

EXERCISE 19A ——————————————————————————

1.
```
      68
  4)272
  -24
    32
   -32
     0
```

2.
```
        21.9
  39)854.1
    -78
     74
    -39
     351
    -351
       0
```

3.
```
       532
  17)9044
    -85
     54
    -51
     34
    -34
      0
```

4.
```
       161.8
  06)970. 8
    -6
     37
    -36
     10
    - 6
      48
     -48
       0
```

Did you make the divisor a whole number? Did you move the decimal point the same number of places in both the divisor and dividend? Did you place the decimal point in the quotient above the decimal point in the dividend?

5. 35.75 ÷ 3.25 = 11   The question asks you to determine the quotient when 35.75 yards of fabric is made into costumes that need 3.25 yards each.

$$
\begin{array}{r}
180 \\
\textbf{6. } 3\overline{)540} \\
-3 \\
\hline
24 \\
-24 \\
\hline
00
\end{array}
\qquad
\begin{array}{r}
30 \\
\textbf{7. } 26\overline{)780} \\
-78 \\
\hline
00
\end{array}
\qquad
\begin{array}{r}
2360 \\
\textbf{8. } 14\overline{)33040} \\
-28 \\
\hline
50 \\
-42 \\
\hline
84 \\
-84 \\
\hline
00
\end{array}
\qquad
\begin{array}{r}
50 \\
\textbf{9. } 204\overline{)10200} \\
-1020 \\
\hline
00
\end{array}
$$

Did you make the divisor a whole number? Did you move the decimal point the same number of places in both the divisor and dividend? Did you place the decimal point in the quotient above the decimal point in the dividend?

10. $21 \div 1.4 = 15$ The question asks you to determine the quotient when a 21 ounce box of cereal is divided into 1.4-ounce servings.

USE WHAT YOU HAVE LEARNED

$$
\begin{array}{r}
34 \\
\textbf{1. } 4\overline{)136} \\
-12 \\
\hline
16 \\
-16 \\
\hline
0
\end{array}
\qquad
\begin{array}{r}
45 \\
\textbf{2. } 194\overline{)6790} \\
-582 \\
\hline
970 \\
-970 \\
\hline
0
\end{array}
\qquad
\begin{array}{r}
160 \\
\textbf{3. } 18\overline{)2880} \\
-18 \\
\hline
108 \\
-108 \\
\hline
00
\end{array}
\qquad
\begin{array}{r}
13.45 \\
\textbf{4. } 52\overline{)699.40} \\
-52 \\
\hline
179 \\
-156 \\
\hline
234 \\
-208 \\
\hline
260 \\
-260 \\
\hline
0
\end{array}
$$

Did you make the divisor a whole number? Did you move the decimal point the same number of places in both the divisor and dividend? Did you place the decimal point in the quotient above the decimal point in the dividend?

5. $35.20 \div .44 = 80$ The question asks you to determine the quotient when 35.2 square feet of floor space uses 8-inch tile with a conversion factor .44.

6. $50.0 \div 4.5 = 11.11$, or 11.11 rounded to the nearest hundredth   The question asks you to determine the quotient when 50 yards of ribbon is made into bows needing 4.5 yards.

7. $\$17.00 \div \$1.13 = 15.044$, or 15.04 rounded to the nearest hundredth The question asks you to determine the quotient when $17.00 is divided into gas that costs $1.13 per gallon.

8. This problem is a multi-step problem. To find how many kits Janice puts together in one hour, divide the number of minutes in an hour (60) by the number of minutes it takes to make one kit (3.33): $60.00 \div 3.33 = 18.018$ or 18.02. To find how much Janice makes in one hour, multiply the number of kits she puts together in one hour (18.02) by the amount of money she makes on each kit (\$.45): $18.02 \times \$.45 = \$8.109$ *or* \$8.11.

9. This problem is a multi-step problem. To find how many centimeters of wire is on a spool, multiply the lengths of the wire (25.5) times 100 centimeters: $25.5 \times 100 = 2,500$. To find how many boards Mike can assemble, divide the length of the wire in centimeters (2,550) by the amount of wire each board takes (12.4): $2,550 \div 12.4 = 205.645$ or 205.65.

10. This problem is a multi-step problem. To find if there are enough bricks for Greg's job, divide the number of bricks (3,861) by the bricks in a square foot (5.5): $3,861 \div 5.5 = 702$. To find out how many more bricks Greg needs, subtract the square footage of bricks available (702) from the total square footage of bricks he needs (820): $820 - 702 = 118$. To find how many more bricks Greg needs, multiply that number times 5.5: $118 \times 5.5 = 649$

LESSON 20 Converting Fractions into Decimals   pages 84–91

EXERCISE 20

1. .33
$$\begin{array}{r} .333 \\ 3\overline{)1.000} \\ -\,9 \\ \hline 10 \\ -\,9 \\ \hline 10 \\ -\,9 \\ \hline 1 \end{array}$$

2.
$$\begin{array}{r} .4 \\ 5\overline{)2.0} \\ -20 \\ \hline 0 \end{array}$$

3. .83
$$\begin{array}{r} .833 \\ 6\overline{)5.000} \\ -48 \\ \hline 20 \\ -18 \\ \hline 20 \\ -18 \\ \hline 2 \end{array}$$

4. .69
$$\begin{array}{r} .687 \\ 16\overline{)11.000} \\ -\,96 \\ \hline 140 \\ -128 \\ \hline 120 \\ -112 \\ \hline 8 \end{array}$$

If necessary, the answer has been rounded to the nearest hundredth. Did you write the numerator as the dividend? Did you write the dividend as a decimal? Did you write the denominator as the divisor? Did you round the number in the hundredths column so it stays the same?

5. $5 \div 8 = .625$ The question asks you to determine how far $\frac{5}{8}$ is using the decimal reading of an odometer.

USE WHAT YOU HAVE LEARNED

1.
$$\begin{array}{r} .8 \\ 5\overline{)4.0} \\ -40 \\ \hline 0 \end{array}$$

2. .43
$$\begin{array}{r} .428 \\ 7\overline{)3.000} \\ -28 \\ \hline 20 \\ -14 \\ \hline 60 \\ -56 \\ \hline 4 \end{array}$$

$$
\begin{array}{r}
6.333 \\
\textbf{3. } 6.33 \quad 6\overline{)38.000} \\
-36 \\
\hline
20 \\
-18 \\
\hline
20 \\
-18 \\
\hline
20 \\
-18 \\
\hline
2
\end{array}
\qquad
\begin{array}{r}
12.555 \\
\textbf{4. } 12.56 \quad 9\overline{)113.000} \\
-\ 9 \\
\hline
23 \\
-18 \\
\hline
50 \\
-45 \\
\hline
50 \\
-45 \\
\hline
50 \\
-45 \\
\hline
5
\end{array}
$$

If necessary, the answer has been rounded to the nearest hundredth. Did you write the numerator as the dividend? Did you write the dividend as a decimal? Did you write the denominator as the divisor? Did you round the number in the hundredths column so it stays the same?

5. $3.00 \div 4 = .75$ The question asks you to determine how to rename $\frac{3}{4}$ as a decimal.

6. $23.00 \div 3 = 7.666$, or 7.67 The question asks you to determine how to rename $7\frac{2}{3}$ as a decimal.

7. This problem is a multi-step problem. Rename each fraction as a decimal: $1\frac{3}{4}$ is $7.00 \div 4 = 1.75$; $\frac{1}{3}$ is $1.00 \div 3 = .333$ or $.33$. To find how many yards Alice will write on the ticket, add both yardage together: $1.75 + .33 = 2.08$. Alice will write the ticket for 2.08 yards.

8. This problem is a multi-step problem. To find the width of the boards, add the two widths together: $1. + 2.75 = 3.75$. Rename the length of the screw $\left(3\frac{1}{2}\right)$ as a decimal: $7.00 \div 2 = 3.5$. 3.5 is shorter than 3.75, so the screw is too short. To find how much too short, subtract the width of the boards (3.75) from the length of the screw (3.5): $3.75 - 3.5 = .25$. The screw is .25 inches too short.

9. This problem is a multi-step problem. Rename the fraction $3\frac{1}{4}$ as a decimal: $13.00 \div 4 = 3.25$. To find how much Ellen charges, multiply the number of miles (3.25) by the cost per $\frac{1}{4}$ mile ($1.25): $3.25 \times \$1.25 = \$4.0625$ or $\$4.06$. Ellen charges $4.06 for the ride.

10. This problem is a multi-step problem. Rename the fraction $2\frac{1}{2}$ as a decimal: $5.0 \div 2 = 2.5$. To find how many steaks Thomas can cut, divide the total weight of the ribeye (21.06) by the weight the customer wants each steak to be (2.5): $21.06 \div 2.5 = 8$ with 1.06 pounds left over. Thomas will cut 8 steaks that are 2.5 pounds and grind 1.06 pounds into hamburger.

EXERCISE A

1.
$$
\begin{array}{r}
3.2 \\
8)\overline{25.6} \\
-24 \\
\hline
16 \\
-16 \\
\hline
0
\end{array}
$$

2.
$$
\begin{array}{r}
12.3 \\
13)\overline{159.9} \\
-13 \\
\hline
29 \\
-26 \\
\hline
39 \\
-39 \\
\hline
0
\end{array}
$$

3.
$$
\begin{array}{r}
14.5 \\
23)\overline{333.5} \\
-23 \\
\hline
103 \\
-92 \\
\hline
115 \\
-115 \\
\hline
0
\end{array}
$$

4.
$$
\begin{array}{r}
14.25 \\
7)\overline{99.75} \\
-7 \\
\hline
29 \\
-28 \\
\hline
17 \\
-14 \\
\hline
35 \\
-35 \\
\hline
0
\end{array}
$$

If you have trouble, refer to Lesson 16.

EXERCISE B

5. 4.58
$$
\begin{array}{r}
4.581 \\
9)\overline{41.230} \\
-36 \\
\hline
52 \\
-45 \\
\hline
73 \\
-72 \\
\hline
10 \\
-9 \\
\hline
1
\end{array}
$$

6. 73.92
$$
\begin{array}{r}
73.916 \\
6)\overline{443.500} \\
-42 \\
\hline
23 \\
-18 \\
\hline
55 \\
-54 \\
\hline
10 \\
-6 \\
\hline
40 \\
-36 \\
\hline
4
\end{array}
$$

If you have trouble, refer to Lesson 16.

EXERCISE C

7.
$$
\begin{array}{r}
200 \\
23)\overline{4600} \\
-46 \\
\hline
000
\end{array}
$$

8.
$$
\begin{array}{r}
19.32 \\
25)\overline{483.00} \\
-25 \\
\hline
233 \\
-225 \\
\hline
80 \\
-75 \\
\hline
50 \\
-50 \\
\hline
0
\end{array}
$$

9.
$$
\begin{array}{r}
200 \\
45)\overline{9000} \\
-90 \\
\hline
000
\end{array}
$$

If you have trouble, refer to Lesson 19.

$$
\begin{array}{r}
375 \\
10.\ 8\overline{)3.000} \\
-24 \\
\hline
60 \\
-56 \\
\hline
40 \\
-40 \\
\hline
0
\end{array}
\qquad
\begin{array}{r}
.66 \\
11.\ 3\overline{)2.00} \\
-18 \\
\hline
20 \\
-18 \\
\hline
2
\end{array}
\qquad
\begin{array}{r}
416 \\
12.\ 12\overline{)5.000} \\
-48 \\
\hline
20 \\
-12 \\
\hline
80 \\
-72 \\
\hline
8
\end{array}
$$

If you have trouble, refer to Lesson 20.

CHAPTER 4 Math at Work

pages 94–97

1. The heart rate is 84 beats per minute. $42 \div .5 = 84$

2. Carla should use 75 pounds of meat. $2.5 \div 6 = .5$ $.5 \times 150 = 75$

3. The regular price of the television is \$208. $156 \div .75 = 208$

4. Bill needs 14.5 square yards of carpet. $12.3 \times 10.6 = 130.38$
   $130.38 \div 9 = 14.4866$ or 14.5

5. The wall is 8 feet long. $12 \div 1.5 = 8$

6. The line is 25 inches long. $20 \times 1.25 = 25$

7. 3.875 pounds. $62 \div 16 = 3.875$

8. It will take Julie 6.25 hours to reach her destination. $250 \div 40 = 6.25$

9. Vincent's patient gets .875 ounces of vitamin supplement today.
   $3.5 \div 4 = .875$

10. The actual bike is 26 inches tall. $3.25 \div .125 = 26$

11. Mark gets 12.8 medium sodas out of a gallon of soda. $16 \div 1.25 = 12.8$

12. Julie could drive 14.5 miles in 15 minutes. $60 \div 4 = 14.5$

13. Bill needs 9.5 pieces of sheet rock. $304.0 \div 32 = 9.5$

14. A bag will feed a horse for 13 days. $100 \div 7.5 = 13.33$ or 13 days rounded to the nearest whole day.

15. Each lot will be 10.12 acres. $80.96 \div 8 = 10.12$

16. Amy earns \$32.06. $4\frac{3}{4} = 4.75$ $6.75 \times 4.75 = 32.0625$, or 32.06 rounded to the nearest hundredth.

17. John can make 31 window screens. $150 \div 4.8 = 31.25$, or 31 rounded to the nearest whole screen.

18. Zeke will pay \$104.25 every three months for insurance.
    $\$409 \div 4 = \$102.25$ $\$102.25 + \$2.00 = \$104.25.$

19. Alicia can make 5 batches of bread. $20.66 \div 4.1 = 5.039$ 5.04, or 5 batches rounded to the nearest complete batch.

20. Each installation should take 3.027 hours. $9.08 \div 3 = 3.027$

21. Elida can groom 5 dogs per day. $8 \div 1.6 = 5$

22. Clara can get 21.019 servings from a can.   85. $81 \div 4.25 = 21.019$ Clara will need 7 cans. $138 \div 21.019 = 6.5654883$, or 7 rounded to the nearest full can.

23. The aisle will be 5 feet wide. $12.5 - 3.75 - 3.75 = 5$
Each side will have 8 dressing rooms. $30 \div 3.75 = 8$.
There will be a total of 16 dressing rooms. $8 \times 2 = 16$

24. The customer will pay \$27.36 each month. $91.19 - 9.11 = 82.08$
$82.08 \div 3 = 27.36$.